The Way of Golf

Robert Brown

Burford Books

Printed in the United States of America

10 9 8 7 6 5 4 3 2 1

Library of Congress Cataloging-in-Publication Data
Brown, Robert A. (Robert Alexander), 1946–
     The way of golf : reconnecting with the soul of the game /
  by Robert Brown.
          p.   cm.
    ISBN 1-58080-081-5 (cloth)
    1. Golf—Psychological aspects.   2. Golf—Moral and ethical
  aspects.   3. Values.   I. Title.
  GV979.P75 B77   2000
  796.352—dc21   00-040318

CONTENTS

I. The Way of Golf

2. Thinking About Golf

3. The Golf Trade

4. Through the Green

5. The Golf Stroke

6. Playing the Game

7. Young Players

8. The 19th Hole

To every golfer who appreciates and plays
by golf's core values—
honesty,
honor,
self-reliance,
playing the course as it is,
playing the ball as it lies—
and tries to do the same in everyday life.

Acknowledgments

This book has been a labor of love. The initial draft was completed in early 1997 and sat maturing in a drawer. As it ripened, I had the idea of creating not just a book, but also a foundation to address the issues of golf's core values—to understand what they were, where they came from, how to teach them, if they were being diluted in any way, and generally to enhance and promote the game's most important elements. I called my friend Malcolm Ferrier, who immediately started pulling together a plan and provided initial financing. The result was Keepers of the Game, officially established in December 1997.

Since then the manuscript has gone through many permutations, guided principally by publisher Peter Burford, who pointed me away from preaching to the choir and toward talking to a larger audience. Peter did a wonderful job editing our first work together, *The Golfing Mind*, and has done a superb job with this one, too. He is also one of the charter members of Keepers of the Game.

Many friends read many versions, among them the aforementioned Malcolm Ferrier, chairman of the board for Keepers of the Game; Jim Corbett, also known as Mr. Golf Etiquette; Martin Farrally, who was the first director of the International Scientific Congress on Golf and is now settled back into running the sports sciences department at the University of St. Andrews; Grant Spaeth, former president of the United States Golf Association; and my brother-in-law Danny Willliams, who represents the avid weekend golfer. All these friends also became charter Keepers members. Two other people should be thanked: Keepers board member Neil Colburn and my good friend and Keepers board member Jim Hay.

In fact, it has been the surge of support for Keepers that has pushed this project along. The ideas and opinions of many who wrote letters and answered our surveys provided considerable grit as I polished the manuscript. However, those who should be thanked most are the special golfers who became charter members of Keepers of the Game. It is these players and organizations that truly support golf and what it should always be. In addition to those already listed, they are:

Robert Swanson
  (the first member)
Bill Stemple
John Ryan
James D. Sykes
Hal Laman
Al Oppenheim
Montana State
  Golf Association
Lauren Pool
Richard Johns
Jim Quigley
Charlie Stein
Dick Jones
Denelle Prouty
P. Chiora
Tony Pancake
Bill Carpenter
Chip Montgomery
Dan Moschetti
Lee Wilcox

Patrick J. Bogard
B. Perry Cormen
Curt Kalmbach
Richard Payne
Greg Hildebrand
Bill Churn
Julia Geolat, RMGCSA
Frank Hardison
Ron Monaco
Joan Shafer
Luke McCormick
David Joy
Eddie Reece
Mike Landers
Steve Collins
Harold Johnston
Darlene Phillips
Grant Ferrier
C. B. Maxwell
Hugh Borthwick
Iain Anderson

Thank you.

Foreword

 I often wonder why golf is so marvelously satisfying.

First would be the endlessly varied experiences, which come in so many ways. The people you get to know from your time together on the course and afterwards. The constantly changing conditions under which you play your shots; the demands of striking the ball the way you want to; the beautiful surroundings. But most of all is the constant understanding you get of yourself, and the ways you become a more complete and civilized person.

These and many other similar topics are addressed in this wonderful book. Bob Brown, a lifetime golfer and an experienced teacher and performance consultant, explores just about all the qualities this great game has to offer. All along the way, he reminds us gently that golf is, above all, a character-building pursuit.

What have I learned over the years on the course? I got to the last green one time—it was at Carnoustie, on the very same green that Jan van de Velde made his memorable seven in the 1999 Open. I, too, needed a par to win a fairly significant (to me, at any rate) national event. I did get nicely over the burns and just off the green in two shots. An easy chip and putt and I was home. But I froze, hit a shabby chip, a worse putt and missed the next one too as I seized up completely. People were sympathetic, but not understanding—"how on earth could you do that?", they asked. I said little, but I sure learnt that you should never comment on anyone's actions unless you have been there yourself. "Never criticize a person unless you have walked in his moccasins" was an old Mohawk motto hanging on my grandma's kitchen wall. So true, and it was golf that taught me that.

Years later, two friends and I went on a golfing holiday. We played for very tiny stakes—just enough to make us take the round with proper seriousness. I nudged my ball on the tenth hole, managed to hit a fine shot, and won that hole. I was pleased—at the time. Later that evening, one of the others said to me "We noticed you moving your ball on the fairway." I was shattered. I had never until then fully realized what a damaging and stupid thing that was to do. I stopped the habit there and then, and have felt much better pleased with myself from the experience. What's the use of winning a dollar or two if you do it in an underhanded way? And I learned something else. It's OK, necessary even, for a friend to step in when it's needed and point out an irregularity. We have responsibilities, learned from golf and applied everywhere, to follow the rules.

As Brown keeps reminding us, golfers experience defining moments of many kinds, but they all have one thing in common: you always learn something useful from them, and they lodge in your character. Golf is undergirded by these character-building occasions, some amusing, some supportive, some offering a tough lesson, all of benefit as something is learned and stored away.

Golf stays with you all your life, and affords differing pleasures as you get older. I'm 70 now, and have finally learned—am still learning—that I should set my own realistic standards. No longer do I get enraged at being a few over par; I'm mighty glad to be able to play, I accept the odd bogey. I don't think I've lowered my ambitions, just set them in line with what is realistic. And that's a salutary thing. Not always the best possible result, but the best result possible.

Now get on and enjoy Bob's fine book. You'll learn a lot about the way of golf. You'll also learn a lot about yourself.

—MALCOLM FERRIER
Chairman, Board of Directors, Keepers of the Game

Introduction

$\mathbf{S}$hooting your age is probably the most satisfying experi-ence in golf. It can come only after considerable effort, many, many rounds of golf, and, of course, reaching a cer-tain honorable sum of years. Those who have accomplished this feat must love the game and have dedicated a substan-tial portion of their lives to the pursuit of understanding golf and coping with its many moods. Thus Joe Cheves should be celebrated among golfers. On August 25, 1999, he toured Mimosa Hills Golf Club in Morganton, North Carolina, a Donald Ross design, in 64 strokes. Joe is 81 years old, so this total was 17 shots less than his age—a new record. Clyde Housel set the old record by shooting 68 at Los Amigos Country Club in Downey, California, when he was 84. Arnold Palmer first shot his age at 66.

Although this milestone is pretty much impossible for most of us, there are many other satisfactions to be gained from playing our good old game. Golf is a lifelong search and, if the search is at all successful, a lifelong series of dis-coveries. Along the way there is testing of limits and, at some point, acceptance of them. There is the wonderment of a difficult shot fully analyzed then well played. There is disappointment and coming back another day to try again. Perhaps best of all, there is spending time with friends or, bittersweet, the comforting memory of those we can never be with again.

I played my first full 18 holes on a real course when I was 11. My dad invited me to play, probably to make up for his failure to invite me to the NFL championship game of

1956—he had two tickets but left me to hear the action on the radio. I shot 121 that first time, and I'm sure I didn't count all my strokes. I can still remember more than 40 years later one lucky chip that smacked into the flag and dropped near the hole for a relatively easy one-putt instead of yet another chip and who knows what.

My dad played, which was one reason I was drawn to golf. But as you know, once you've hit a shot high in the air and seen it land anywhere close to where you aimed, golf grabs quick and holds tight. Sometime before I graduated from high school my dad and I played a memorable round together. On a short par-5 I managed a straight tee shot, a very long (for me) 3-wood, and—probably for the first time in my life—had a putt for an eagle. My father held the flag waiting for me to putt. It was one of those umpteen-hundred-foot putts. No chance to make it, little chance to get it close. I hit and hoped. Rolling up, down, around, and seemingly endlessly, the ball ran and ran and finally dropped into the cup. I'll forever remember my father's exuberant smile. He threw up his hands and cried, "Birdie." "No," I said, "eagle!" My father's genuine joy at my supposed birdie multiplied my even more astounded joy at a real eagle. The joy was tainted when my father didn't realize it was for eagle and I had to justify how I'd managed to be putting for three. Still, it was at that moment that I had my first experience of how golf gives and takes at the same time—an inkling that golf was much, much more than just a game.

Years later I wanted to test myself in U.S. Open qualifying tournaments. At that time a player had to be a 2-handicap or less to get in. I practiced every day, mostly on my short game, and played at least once or twice a week to get my scores low enough. I was a 3 at the deadline and a 2-handicap a month too late. Not long after that I experienced one of many golf revelations. I was consulting with the Craft-Zavichas Golf School and playing a casual round with two of the instructors. On a par-5, one of the very long-hitting instructors and I were lying two, almost equally distant from the green. The pro asked me what I was going to hit. Assuming he was thinking I'd take too little club, I told him "pitching wedge" and further explained that the wedge would ensure that I got over the bunker. The pro, whose shot was a few yards shorter than mine, said, "I'm hitting a 9."

"A 9!" I was sure my pitching wedge was too much club and, until I'd been asked, had intended to play a sand wedge. "Why a 9?" I was incredulous.

"With a 9 I can make sure I'm over the bunker, and if I cut it a little bit I can go around the bunker and spin it toward the hole."

It was then, as a two handicap, that I fully understood how much I had to learn—and it would probably take me more than a lifetime. It was perhaps at that moment I fell in love with the game.

In the early 1990s I was lucky enough to become an honorary reader at the University of St. Andrews. There I completed a book on the mental game, had the delight of teaching golf to university students and citizens of the town, and spent many wonderful afternoons sitting outside the golf shop watching players on the first tee and last green of the Old Course. A few times I played the ancient links alone, many times with good friends. In this setting golf seeped into my every pore.

This book is an exploration into golf, deep inside its workings and deep inside its players. There are hundreds of books intended to help golfers swing better and hundreds featuring pictures of beautiful golf courses from around the world. This book is different. I wanted to write a book that would help every player better appreciate the game, one that would add the perspective that otherwise comes only with decades of experience and listening to the wisdom of enlightened golfers.

Golf is special. Many golfers are special. I fear, however, that golf will not always be the same game it is now. Many forces are pulling at it. Commercialization is one, societal norms are another. Traditions are becoming disposable. Standards are ceasing to exist. The core values of golf, honor, honesty, self-reliance, and playing the course and the ball as you find them, are being lost. They are being replaced by what is easy and fun, in the same way that fast food and television have replaced the family sitting together at the dinner table.

I don't know what is significant in golf. All I know is that the hours spent playing golf have been a time of supreme enjoyment for me, whether I was playing alone, with friends, or with strangers. I know that fixing divots on the fairway and repouring ball marks on the green connects me to the game and the golfers playing after me. I know that golf makes me think of my father, his trademark fade, our mutual excitement at his first hole-in-one after 40 years of golf, and our walks together down so many fairways. I know that golf reminds me of wonderful holidays and countless chats in convivial 19th holes. I know that some of my happiest times are when my wife and I play nine holes together carrying only 5-irons in the summer twilight before sharing appetizers and wine. I hope my children will play. I hope that golf will be the same for my grandchildren as it has been for me.

The Way of Golf defines the game as I and some others see it. There is no guarantee that the game we love will last another 50 years, let alone another 500. I believe it needs stewardship. I believe the best people to provide guidance are those who know and love the game and have the right perspective. This book is my contribution to that perspective.

No matter how much or how little you agree with what I've written, recognize that the game of golf is your responsibility. You are one of the players who defines what it will be—whether it will remain the extraordinary game that it has been and should always be.

1

THE WAY OF GOLF

The Ancient and Honorable Pastime

Discovered along the rugged seaside of Scotland, golf was shaped by gentlemen—honorable and dedicated men who soon became passionate about their walks through the swales and mounds of the countryside. It is a game of strict honesty, passed down from father to son, mother to daughter, a birthright and an obligation. For 500 years golf has exposed and created character. It's played by kings and presidents, clerks and cooks, and today's players have inherited its destiny.

The game is reputed to be so easy that a child can play it, and so difficult that it cannot be learned in a lifetime. Many have tried to describe the nature of golf, none more simply and clearly than Herbert Warren Wind in the introduction to his book *Following Through*:

> [Golf] is the only [game] played on natural terrain or on grounds made to resemble gently rolling linksland. It is the one outdoor game in which a stationary player hits a stationary ball. The fact that a player must generate his own power is one of the fundamental reasons that golf is perhaps the most difficult of all the major games to play consistently well. For one reason or another, golf seems to provide more fun and humor than any other game, and yet at the same time it has achieved the finest body of literature of any game. And golf has been a lucky game. It has been blessed with admirable champi-

ons and, decade after decade, this has renewed the high standards of sportsmanship and the pleasurable atmosphere associated with it.

Golf is a test, a complicated, difficult, and ever-changing examination. It is frustrating; at times you'll wonder why you bother with all the aggravation. Like a lover, golf teases, seduces, gives, takes, surprises, torments, comforts, and overwhelms. We love golf, and strange as it may sound—golf seems to give love back.

Yet we treat the game with less regard than a poor cousin. Natural terrain is pushed and shoved into a designer's image of market appeal. Golf-club innovations hit the showroom floor with the regularity of the lunar cycle. Spectators get up close and personal with taunts and jeers. A significant number of courses require players to ride along the sides of fairways in miniature automobiles, while an equally frightening number charge three-digit green fees.

Golf is expected to be every man's game, to be socially responsible and environmentally friendly, to grow despite competition from computer games and video rentals, to build character when today's athletes are as likely to win parole as a game, and to fit our lifestyle when four hours seems like a lifetime. Should the game be kept as is, or does golf require modernization?

It's as if golfers have been bequeathed a cherished yet burdensome heirloom, like a rustic, centuries-old cottage. Do we preserve this grand old thing that just might be a white elephant? How much can we knock down walls, add a low-flow toilet or two, and put in new lighting before the old charm disappears? Should experts be hired to design something up to date? This book explores all of these issues and provides one solution: Dedicated players should do all they can to preserve, enhance, and promote the game's core values.

For five centuries golf's primary competition has been match play, one player against another or two against two. Face to face—an intimate battle of skill and heart. The basic rule was "fair and equitable"—an absolute necessity in this game of ill winds, bad bounces, and the rub of the green. From such contests arose the core values of honor, honesty, self-reliance, etiquette, and playing the ball and the course as they were found. It is these values from its earliest days that make golf the ancient and honorable pastime. Golf is too noble to let slide into the ordinary.

Golf isn't a reaction game, like football, baseball, or tennis, one of trained reflexes responding to a moving ball. Golf demands a considered response and comes with a promise that even the right response may not be successful. There is no defense. No place to hide. No running out the clock. No quitting even if defeat is inevitable. For centuries these elements of golf have been associated with character.

In golf anything can happen. Arnold Palmer in the 1966 U.S. Open and Greg Norman at Augusta thirty years later were helpless against the inherent despair of the game. Superb golfers, both lost insurmountable leads—the death rattle impossible to quiet. Such experiences are like being wounded in battle, straining to comprehend how the pain, the horror, the destruction could be happening. "Why can't I stop this?"

Even victory can be bittersweet. Nick Faldo added the jewel of the Masters Golf Tournament to his major-titles crown when Norman faltered. Poor Nick Faldo. No one, except maybe Nick and his caddie, will remember how precisely he dissected the fairways and how wisely he placed his ball on the treacherous greens. Instead, all the world will remember how Norman lost his six-stroke lead, fell behind another five, and was fortunate to finish second.

A smaller event saw a smaller misfortune, but one characteristic of golf as well. Andrew Morse put his approach shot close to the hole on the last green of the 1983 Massachusetts Open. A simple two-putt par would have made him the first amateur in almost 30 years to win this tournament. But the young man failed to replace his ball properly, was assessed a two-stroke penalty, and ended up tied for second. It is a cruel game, and not always a fair one.

The wonder of golf is its self-imposed agony. The problem is laid out before your eyes. There is plenty of time to analyze and plan. The ball doesn't twist and dive but patiently waits for you to send it on its way, sometimes from atop a wooden peg. Fourteen clubs sit in the bag to be picked over and carefully chosen. No one is going to rush up and tackle you from behind. The game is played in a park-like setting, at a leisurely pace, with cool drinks only steps away. You can sit and rest whenever you wish. There is even a map, measured and subdivided into edible bites. Everything is in your favor. You couldn't ask for better conditions to ensure success. It is almost unfair.

But playing golf is like meeting the devil, who presents in one open hand happiness, excitement, and joy beyond our wildest dreams while at the same time twisting and crushing our souls within the other gnarled and ugly fist.

A 280-yard drive that's 1 inch out of bounds costs an extra stroke and a long walk back to the tee to hit again. A complete whiff counts only the stroke taken. A 2-foot birdie putt knocked off line by a spike mark erases a long drive down the middle, a 3-wood through a narrow opening in the trees, and a sand wedge that carried over a pot bunker and spun back 15 feet. People say it's unfair, as if that condemns what it is.

Golf is only a game. It isn't required to be fair, only interesting. For a game to be worthwhile it must offer an engaging challenge and a degree of reward and pleasure in its playing. Golf does that and so much more.

Golf is only a game, but its features test every part of your character. And it's not much of a stretch to believe that the golfer who plays the game the way it should be played also exhibits stellar human qualities beyond the boundaries of the course. It is a game rich in its demands and generous in its rewards.

There is something wonderful about it that reaches all the senses, like the beauty of a well-struck putt rolling through early-morning dew. Golfers have favorite places to play, professionals who must be followed, even a favorite club or two in the bag. Shots from 20 years ago are remembered as if they were struck yesterday. Even entire rounds can be replayed in our heads while we sit in an easy chair, eyes closed, and with a happy sigh each time the ball clicks off the clubface or plops into the cup. Golf has captured its players like this for over five centuries.

What makes golf the attraction it is? According to A. A. Milne, "It is the best game in the world at which to be bad." Psychologists might postulate that it is the risk and the occasional reward that stimulate us, the same mechanisms that draw us to the one-armed bandits in Las Vegas. Others might mention the parklike setting, being outdoors, the ever-changing conditions, the easy pace, the companionship, or the joy that comes from a well-hit shot.

A. J. Balfour in 1890 put it this way:

> A tolerable day, a tolerable green, a tolerable opponent, supply, or ought to supply, all that any reasonably constituted human being should require in the way of entertainment. With a fine sea view, and a clear course in front of him, the golfer should find no difficulty in dismissing all worries from his mind, and regarding golf, even if it may be very indifferent golf, as the true and adequate end of man's existence. Care may sit behind the horseman, she never presumes to walk with the caddie. No inconvenient reminiscences of the ordinary workaday, no internals of weariness or monotony interrupt the pleasures of the game. And of what other recreation can this be said?

Michael Murphy expresses a similar view through the golfer's wife Agatha McNaughton in *Golf in the Kingdom:*

> Golf is for smellin' heather and cut grass and walkin' fast across the countryside and feelin' the wind and watchin' the sun go down and seen' your friends hit good shots and hittin' some yerself. It's love and it's feeling the splendour o' this good world.

There is a sense of connectedness in golf—to the elements, to fellow players, and to the heritage of the game. Today's weekend player can literally walk over the old stone bridge in the footsteps of Allen Robertson, the first professional at St. Andrews, or attempt the chip Tom Watson sank at Pebble Beach to win the U.S. Open. There is joy in the play. Is there anything more rewarding than rifling a 5-iron through a stiff crosswind and watching it curve through the air just as you planned, hit the front of the green, and roll close to the hole? There is despair, too, of course, and the eternal hope that the next shot will bring out that swing you know waits inside. It is a constant puzzle, and rewarding as no other game.

Remember that first time you beat your mom or dad? Such events can be remembered for a lifetime. Magical things can happen. The entire golfing world was agog at the 1977 British Open. Tom Watson and Jack Nicklaus dueled over Turnberry as if they were swordfighting over the rolling deck of a pirate ship. It was thrust and parry between them as if the rest of the world didn't exist. Tom shot 65, 65 the last two rounds to scuttle Jack, who shot 65, 66. Both made birdie at the last hole. Third-place holder Hubert Green was a distant 11 shots behind, shaking his head and mumbling as he left the course that the other two guys had somehow skipped three or four holes.

Speaking of Nicklaus, the spirit of golf soared during the 1969 Ryder Cup at Royal Birkdale. On the final hole of the match Nicklaus made his difficult 5-footer and immediately picked up Tony Jacklin's marker. "I am sure you would hole that putt," he told the Brit, "and I'm not prepared to see you miss." A Jacklin miss and the United States would have won the Ryder Cup outright. Jack's gesture squared their match—and the entire cup competition—at 16 points each. U.S. captain Sam Snead was hopping mad, but the golf world rejoiced at the sportsmanship.

No one knows how golf started. Many cultures have played games with sticks and balls. Back in the days of the Caesars Romans played a game with a ball stuffed with feathers. After the Dark Ages Germans played games similar to golf, as did the Chinese before the Scots wore clothes, let alone kilts. Professor Ling Hongling from the University of Lanzhow, China, has found line drawings on Sung dynasty pottery showing players hitting balls into a hole with curved sticks. Exactly when one or more of these games evolved into what we know of as golf is open to debate, and there is little likelihood of finding agreement or confirming documentation. Holland can claim the first visual records of a game that resembles golf, while the earliest written reference to actual golf was in 1457, when King James II decreed during the 14th Parliament in Edinburgh that "Fute Ball and Golfe be utterly cryed dwone." Not long after, James IV took up the game.

It appears that Holland saw the birth of a popular game of hitting a ball to objects, like doorjambs and hitching posts, while the Scots refined this game into what we now play—hitting the ball into a specified number of holes and counting the number of strokes it takes to do so. The ties between the two countries were close. Examining a map reveals that all the early British golf courses clung to the east coast of Scotland, a quick sail from the Netherlands. The kingdom of Fife and the medieval town of St. Andrews stick out from the island nation like a swollen thumb.

The most ancient of golf courses, the Old Course at St. Andrews, was first played over 500 years ago. The town is at least another 500 years older than that, with an organized government created in 1141. The cathedral was founded in 1160, the castle begun in 1200, and St. Andrews University established in 1411. It is a delightful old place of crumbling stone walls and chilly winds off the gray North Sea.

The Old Course was first called that when a new course was constructed alongside it. The "New Course" was built and named in the 1890s. Much of this hallowed ground is natural, sculpted by rain, wind, and animals. A few humans had a hand in enhancing the land for golf, most notably Old Tom Morris, who became "Old Tom" when his son was born. At one time the course played to 22 holes—11 out and 11 in.

There is evidence in the St. Andrews University Library that at least one hole was up the hill near what is currently the Martyrs' Monument, a direct niblick through where the Royal and Ancient Clubhouse now stands. By 1764 the first 4 holes had been deemed too short (does that sound familiar?) and were made into 2, as were the last 4 holes for a total of 18. Other courses at the time had different numbers. Leith in Edinburgh had 5 holes, Musselburgh nearby had 7, while Montrose and Aberdeen had 25. By the early 1800s St. Andrews's prestige had so grown that other clubs followed the 18-hole standard. Then, as Scots are wont to do, they traveled overseas and the game went with them.

Golf was played in some form in America before the United States was born, brought to the South Carolina area in the mid-1700s. However, most people date U.S. golf to the establishment of the St. Andrews Golf Club in Yonkers, New York, in 1888.* It wasn't much of a course—three holes cut into rough cow pasture—but it saw the beginning of continuous play in the U.S. Today an estimated 25 million Americans play 500 million rounds a year on over 15,000 courses. Worldwide the game is played by twice that number of people, from preschoolers all the way to those who are able to shoot their age and better.

---

*Lorne Rubinstein reminds me that golf began in Canada at the Royal Montreal Golf Club in 1873.

That Kind of People

Who are golf's 50 million players? Where did they come from—where are they going—and what are they like?

It's easy to imagine that golfers in the early days were simply men in the fields who had a moment's free time and the inclination to swipe at a loose stone. Since ball games were common in towns and villages, it wouldn't have taken long for a couple of men to challenge one another to a test of skill. And it takes no stretch of the imagination to conclude that early forms of golf were spontaneous pastimes of farmers, herders, children—everyone who found himself outdoors and a little bored.

Golf was an informal game, played with equipment of considerable variety. Whatever was at hand was good enough.

At least a few enjoyed the game enough to do two things: fashion a club to be used, stored away, and brought out again and again; and play over a plot of land they favored and would return to again and again.

Golf remained an informal pastime until the 18th century, when an emerging middle class formed organizations to better enjoy camaraderie and a bit of sport. In 1754, 22 men of Fife joined together into what they called "The Society of St. Andrews Golfers." Of them three were earls, two were sons of an earl (one in Parliament), two were knights, one a lieutenant general, one a member of Parliament, two professors at St. Andrews University, and one the provost; the rest were a smattering of lairds and merchants. Across the Firth of Forth another group at Muirfield—

the "Honourable Company of Edinburgh Golfers"—also banded together and even compiled a list of rules. Once these men got hold of things, equipment became standardized, meetings and matches were scheduled well in advance, and (naturally), the links had to be managed rather than simply left to the elements and the whims of the townspeople.

Old St. Andrews is a case in point. In 1801 George Cheape sent a letter to the St. Andrews town council complaining that the links were being destroyed by rabbits. It seems a Charles Dempster had purchased the links land and surrounding parcels from the Earl of Kellie. Mr. Dempster, who raised rabbits, also declared that dogs were not allowed on his links and went so far as to lay down traps and poison. The conflicts began on the links in the form of pushing matches, and in town with equally heated council debates. By 1806 the case had found its way to the House of Lords.

The end result was that a man was hired to keep the links in good shape, and Mr. Cheape (Cheape's bunker can be found protecting the green that serves the 2nd and 16th holes on the Old Course) bought the links and arranged to give the then Golfing Society the "privilege of the golfing ground."

Golf was at a crossroads, and it took two paths. One was toward organization and formality, with men of rank controlling the playing ground. These men of means wore uniforms when they played. They competed for silver cups and crystal bowls, and paid fines to fellow members with a bottle or two of claret. The other path was the status quo. Men who had little free time and even less money played with home-fashioned equipment on any available patch of land, including the common links. They played when the whim came upon them and with implements "ill suited to the task."

This wasn't to say the game was any less difficult or challenging when played by the upper crust. The autumn 1860 meeting at St. Andrews was notable for two events: first a fierce gale that hammered the links, town, and sea, and second a vessel in distress in the bay. Few townsmen wanted to risk their lives manning the lifeboat. Maitland Dougall, who was scheduled to play in the medal, took an oar and fought against the sea for five hours in the successful rescue. He returned, bored a hole in his guttie, filled it with buckshot to keep it low, and won the Golf Medal by shooting 112. As an aside, nine years earlier the contest had been played in similarly abysmal weather; the winner scored 105 by using his putter for every shot.

Throughout this period golf was dominated by those of class and wealth. As the game emigrated to the New World it came to be controlled less by class and more by wealth. Still, in both cases golf was a refined pastime—a sporting event for the genteel—a game of intellect rather than brawn. The customs and etiquette of the game reflected the standards of the club members. It was a gentleman's game, although a few ladies were grudgingly allowed to participate.

During the era when women wore many layers of clothing and assorted support items and tended to swoon, golf was seen as a way for the weaker sex to get healthful but not-too-strenuous exercise. The self-control the game demanded was also an excellent way to bolster always-unsteady female nerves. The prevailing attitude, obviously, was condescension. One observer near the close of the 19th century noted, "If [women] choose to play . . . when the male golfers are feeding or resting, no one can object . . . at other times . . . they are in the way." An entry in the complaints register of the Worcestershire Golf Club expressed the attitude with unmistakable clarity: "I noticed a lady in the clubhouse at the weekend. I urge the Secretary to see that this does not happen again."

Professional golfers weren't treated with much respect early on, either. They were tradesmen, after all. In the earliest days they made bows and arrows and the occasional golf club. As the game became more popular, ball making was added—stuffing and pounding leather and feathers into the old featherie. By the early 1800s a few men in Scotland were able to earn a living solely from club and ball making. Once golfing societies were formed, a few of these men added greenkeeping to their tasks.

Allen Robertson of St. Andrews is probably the first of the breed that today we call golf professionals. Robertson was born in 1815 and died in 1859. He was employed by the Royal and Ancient to keep the green, but was better known as the best player of his time. He was victorious in many money matches, often the partner of Old Tom Morris. Robertson did it all: made the best featheries, went around the Old Course in 79, and tutored the most inept into loving the game. The Reverend W. W. Tulloch wrote that Robertson "was the most outstanding figure and the most interesting personality in any links in the first half of the nineteenth century."

One of the most celebrated players of the next century was an amateur, Bobby Jones. Bob, as he much preferred being called, probably described golf and golfers best when he said that golf "is usually played with the outward appearance of great dignity. It is nevertheless, a game of considerable passion, either of the explosive type or that which burns inwardly and sears the soul."

Bob Jones exhibited both. He was known and even notorious for his temper in his younger days. Alex Smith, a Scottish professional, proclaimed that Jones would never make it as a golfer; "tae much temper," he said. And Jones, of course, forever regretted tearing up his scorecard as he was about to take a six on the par-3 11th hole during the third round of the 1921 British Open at St. Andrews. He did not walk off the course, as many have heard, but he had no scorecard to turn in after the round. Jones did manage a 72 in the final, although unofficial, round.

Later that year in the U.S. Amateur, Jones was one down at the 35th hole to Willie Hunter, who was on the green. Jones skulled his approach over the green and, in a rage, threw his club, hitting a woman spectator. George Walker (President Bush's grandfather and the Walker of that international amateur competition, the Walker Cup) was then president of the United States Golf Association. He sent the gentleman from Georgia a letter: "You will never play in a USGA event again unless you learn to control your temper."

Throughout his playing career it seemed to Jones that it was "such an utterly useless and idiotic thing to stand up to a perfectly simple shot, one that I know I can make a hundred times running without a miss—and then mess up the blamed thing, the one time I want to make it! And it's gone forever—an irrevocable crime."

That is the nature of golf and golfers. You stand alone, totally exposed, totally responsible. Because golf allows plenty of time to consider the shot, because you have no one else to either rely on or blame, because results are clearly evident, and because there is so much time for introspection during play, you can experience all the vicissitudes of life over the span of 18 holes.

Sometimes emotions can swing from rage to joy in less than a second. Brent Maynard, a weekend golfer in San Diego, was struggling through a round at the Coronado municipal course bothered by both an uncontrollable slice and the group behind him, which was repeatedly hitting early. His tee ball would go right, and the following group's tee balls would whiz by before he had a chance to hit his second. Brent isn't a slow player, but he's a polite one, and he did his best to ignore the situation while figuring out his banana ball. Still, his frustration grew. Midway through the back nine he was about to play his second when a tee ball from behind hit him in the calf. Without thinking, he whirled around and smacked the ball back toward the tee with his 5-iron. The ball went deep, sailing almost all the way back, the trajectory high with the hint of a draw. Instantly his anger was gone, replaced by a look of happy astonishment. Brent rushed over to his playing companion, the other foursome forgotten. "You know," he said, "I kept my right elbow in. All I had to do was keep my elbow in. Isn't that great!"

Most golfers are like Brent, on a never-ending quest for improvement. Gadgets, quick fixes, different balls, different clubs (especially putters and drivers), tips in magazines, in newspapers, and from friends all become part of the search for 10 more yards and five less strokes. Equipment manufacturers are quick to meet the need. The first great leap of technology for the golfer's benefit was the discovery of the gutta-percha ball, which replaced the featherie.

The story, perhaps true, is that in 1843 a black marble idol of Vishnu was sent by a medical missionary from Burma to Dr. Paterson of St. Andrews University. The packing material was a fascinating malleable substance that was stored away for later investigation. A couple of years had passed when Dr. Paterson's son Robert made a golf ball from the material and played the Old Course like never before. The new ball was durable, cheap, and repairable: After use, you just heated it up and re-formed it. The only problem was that new balls tended to dive and drop quickly when hit. With experience, golfers learned to nick the surface so the ball would stay airborne better. With such accessible and improved equipment, the game was again within reach of common folks.

One invention didn't turn out so well. After the guttie was supplanted by the Haskell ball in 1906, the Goodyear company tried to capture the market with a rubber shell filled with compressed air. Using the ball in an exhibition in New York, Willie Dunn sliced into the gallery. A woman spectator was injured when the ball exploded.

A bit safer and much more subtle than exploding golf balls are today's efforts to improve players' minds. Nerves have always been a problem, but until recently the jitters were accepted as simply part of the game. During the third round of the 1953 Masters tournament, for instance, British amateur champion John DeForest put his approach to the 13th into the creek fronting the green. After contemplating his options, DeForest decided to play the ball from the water. He carefully took off one shoe and sock, and rolled up his pant leg. He took one more look at his target, then stepped into the water—planting his bare foot safely on dry land. Without a flinch, he played out.

Then there was Ty Caplin, who was about to tee off in the first round of the 1966 U.S. Open. He insisted he wasn't nervous, "not at all. I just forgot to put on my shoes," he said.

It's that kind of game.

All golfers who play more than just an occasional round eventually become immersed in a series of defining moments, and perhaps one or two critical ones. Possibly the most significant contributor to defining moments is golf's reliance on self-policing—on honor. For most players, there are no referees or representatives from the USGA or R&A or any other organization observing play with rulebook in hand. Most often, in fact, there is no one but you. Everyone who has played golf more than just a few times and has some knowledge of the rules has had to face the decision of calling a self-imposed penalty—or not. The first few times this situation occurs, a young player usually leans toward score rather than honor. It would be a rare kid who'd give up a stroke or two just to obey an abstract concept like the ball moving at address. With experience, however, and looking in the mirror, you begin to understand yourself and the game. As you mature and learn about more important human characteristics than ego, love of and respect for the game enable a quick yet decisive choice to do what is honorable, even when no one is looking. This, perhaps more than anything else, differentiates the golfer from others. Duty to the game supersedes fun or shooting a good score; violations are acknowledged even if it breaks your heart. This perspective makes the game and its players special.

Part of this perspective comes from having no one to blame but yourself when things go wrong. Everyone has a personal golf disaster story, few as poignant as that of Len Mattiace, a young professional playing the final round of the Players Championship. He had a chance to win as he faced the tee shot over the water at the infamous island par-3 17th. Looking on was his mother, sitting in a wheelchair, severely ill with cancer. Mattiace, however, hit two balls into the water, eventually finishing the hole with a quintuple-bogey eight. The tournament was lost. His disappointment must have been monumental. However, he kept his head up; no club slamming, no cursing, no giving up. He birdied the last hole and finished second. Was there heartbreak? No. His mother said, "He didn't win . . . but he's a winner." She died without seeing him play another tournament.

Could this occur anywhere but in golf? The scene is a retirement village in Winter Haven, Florida. Twice-a-week league play. Resident Donald DeGreve collapses while putting on the 16th green. Resuscitation fails and he dies. While the other members of his foursome quit to inform his widow, paramedics cover the body with a sheet and await permission to remove the body. The rest of the league golfers play through. Not quite the old joke of "hit the ball—drag Fred,"* but the players all realized that it could have been any one of them. Most thought it was not a bad way to go.

It's that kind of game and golfers are that kind of people.

---

*It's a golf joke long in the tooth, but you may not have heard it. Trevor played every Tuesday after work and was home, regular as clockwork, in time for dinner. Except one particular Tuesday. His wife was worried, as dinnertime was long past. Finally the exhausted man came through the door. "What happened?" his wife asked. "It was horrible," Trevor told her. "Fred collapsed early in the round." His wife gasped. "You went to the hospital?" Trevor shook his head. "No, no. Poor Fred was dead. That's what took so long. For the next 11 holes it was hit the ball—drag Fred. Hit the ball—drag Fred."

Traditions

Golfers and golf have a long history, one that has produced a considerable tradition, some of it good, some bad. Part of the golfer's heritage includes unwritten rules—for instance, the winner of the match buys refreshments at the 19th hole. One well-known but little-experienced tradition is that anyone lucky enough to score a hole-in-one buys drinks. Originally this might have meant buying drinks for the foursome or anyone who observed the shot. In some places, today, it means buying drinks for whoever is in the bar when you get there. Japanese golfers have extended the lucky golfer's obligation. There, the custom is to buy gifts after the happy event for friends who play golf. Someday the hapless hole-in-one-er may have to buy gifts for golfing friends *and* friends who one day may play golf.

Another tradition is called "the snake." Often used as a betting tool as well as a symbol of ineptitude, the first player to three-putt is given ownership of the snake, usually made of rubber, but sometimes only a figurative concept. The owner of the snake broods and moans until another in the group falls victim to a three-putt. It is often said that golfers don't wish ill on other golfers, but that is rarely, if ever, the case with the snake.

Another tradition that has a downside is the "honor" of the low scorer on a hole playing first. It's a small thing, but sometimes burdensome, for the worst-playing golfer to always tee off last. Not only does that player face following better tee shots, but he often ends up hitting in front of an audience when the players behind are making their way to the tee. Although "ready golf"—in which whoever is ready hits—can speed up play somewhat, there is at least one other reason to play that way: The person playing badly can get it over with quicker—miss it quick, as Lee Trevino used to say.

The traditional wager in Britain is a ball. Lose the match, you hand your opponent a new golf ball. This certainly keeps the game in perspective.

One wonderful, highly restricted tradition that most of us will never enjoy is the Champion's Dinner held just before competition begins at the Masters every April. Here, past champions dine on a menu chosen by the prior year's winner (the menu has ranged from haggis to barbecue). Imagine sitting at a long table having a chat with Nicklaus, Palmer, Snead, Crenshaw, Woods, or the pro emeritus Byron Nelson. In 1999 Gene Sarazen, Snead, and Nelson were the honorary starters for the tournament, each hitting off the first tee. At age 97, Sarazen hit his down the middle.

First-tee jitters are often evident at the captain's "playing himself in" at St. Andrews when he hits off the first tee to the accompaniment of a booming cannon immediately to his right. With townspeople and members of the club looking on, caddies line up near the expected landing area to snag the ball. The lucky one who returns it is, by tradition, awarded a gold sovereign. Many captains have played themselves in with the caddies waiting disrespectfully close by.

Some of golf's traditions are so common we're barely aware of them. Using a tee to start a hole hails back to the days when wet sand was taken from the bottom of the hole and made into a small mound on which the ball was placed. This was done when the rules required driving off within two club lengths of the hole just completed. On the rare occasions when *fore* has to be yelled out after a wild shot, we could be using the modern version of the gentlemanly *to the fore* of 100 years ago. *Fore* could be a portion of *before* or even the sailory *fore* as in *fore and aft*.

Even playing in groups of four is based on the traditional match-play game of foursomes in which two golfers play one ball in alternate shots against two others. This game is still played in Britain and in international matches like the Ryder Cup.*

Such traditions connect us with the past. Yet tradition on its own has no value. It is simply something common to prior generations and as such may hinder development. The American Professional Golfers Association actually had a Caucasians-only clause written into its by-laws, belatedly erased in the 1960s. Some private clubs today discriminate against those they don't want to associate with, which is what being private is all about, but they do so with significant and narrow-minded bias. Unfortunately, this is part of golf's heritage, too.

Walking is customary. There were certainly no carts in the early days, even for the gentry of the Honourable Company. The Casey Martin situation, in which a talented yet disabled golfer could compete only if allowed to ride a cart, raised the issue of the tradition of walking versus the common modern practice of motoring in carts. Is walking an integral part of the game? Is it a tradition of no importance? Is golf one game that can be played at the highest level by the disabled with a little help?

Caddies were once common, then became a dying breed, and now seem to be coming back from near-extinction. The chance for a boy or girl to earn some money, get some exercise, enjoy the outdoors, and spend time with adults seems too good to let go, especially for kids who are starting life with disadvantages.

"Play the course as you find it" used to be a tradition. Now it has become, "If it ain't as green as Augusta, it's a goat

---

*An American tourist once pleaded with the then (infamous) secretary Paddy Hanmer of Muirfield. He wanted to play the famous course—which was empty—had all the references and was ready to go. The secretary looked him up and down shaking his head. "No," he said. "You're an American. You'll play too slow. I have a foursome match beginning in two hours and you'll be in their way."

trail." The Golf Course Superintendents Association of America blames television for this attitude—as does Dr. Mike Kenna, director of the USGA's Green Section. "It started when people turned on their televisions and they weren't black and white anymore," he says. "Golfers got smart real fast; they wanted that dark green color they saw on television." Mike Wallace, superintendent at Hop Meadow Country Club in Simsbury, Connecticut, agrees. "Members' demands are driven by what they see on TV. They'll see a spectacular course that's been set up for one week, and then they want to have that the whole golfing season." So when conditions are not ideal, winter rules are invoked (as soon as Thanksgiving in some places, and there is some irony there): Scores don't count toward handicap from November through March, and unplayable lies can occur everywhere.*

A tradition still in good standing is kindness. Golfers do not jeer one another. The loser congratulating the winner is usually sincere, even if disappointed. Standing so you are not in the line of sight of the one hitting and making sure your shadow isn't a distraction are automatic to experienced players. So is saying "good shot." Greg Norman did nothing unusual for a golfer during the 1998 President's Cup in Australia. While waiting for partner Steve Elkington to hit, he walked over to two kids sitting in wheelchairs in the shade of a tree and autographed team flags and baseball caps for them. They didn't speak, but smiled and gave the thumbs-up sign. "You got it, mate," Norman said as he returned to play.

Opponents help each other look for lost balls. Competitors confer with one another about the rules. One can give the okay to another to remove a ball from play. All are charged with protecting the field.

---

*One benchmark of where things are headed was the preparation of Congressional Country Club for a recent U.S. Open. The fairways were mowed with walking green mowers, cutting the fairways to the same speed greens were 20 years earlier.

On the recreational level, no game provides more chance for socializing. Two players deep in conversation have been known to forget to hit their approach shots and wind up on the green confused, then embarrassed.

One of golf's more enjoyable traditions is finishing the round with your playing companions, sampling your favorite beverage, and reliving the highs and lows of the match. The fellow who did this the best it could ever be done was J. Wood Platt, a member at Pine Valley, one of the toughest courses anywhere. He was a very talented amateur golfer but even better at recognizing reality. He began his round one day by putting his 4-iron second shot close enough for a birdie on the first hole. His approach to the elevated second was even better: His 7-iron found the hole for an eagle two. Platt was three under after only two holes. Pine Valley's third is a 185-yard par-3. Platt holed-in-one to go five under after three holes. He cooled off at the fourth, a par-4 of 461 yards. His 4-wood second shot found the green but was 30 feet from the hole. Rusty after attempting only one putt up until then, Platt still managed to sink his effort for yet another birdie. Six under after four holes. Great golf, but now he showed real genius. The clubhouse bar is close by the path from the fourth green to the fifth tee. Mr. Platt entered the bar and did not return to his game.

Human traditions can be anachronisms, they can be connections to the past, they can provide a sense of belonging, and they can be used to exclude. Golf traditions are no different. Make what you will of them, they have evolved as a way for people to make a pleasant pastime more meaningful. If a golfer keeps his shirt on when the day gets hot, he is following a long tradition of gentlemanly conduct. If another golfer digs a divot and walks on without replacing it, he is ignoring part of his responsibility to the game and other players.

Perhaps the greatest tradition in golf is largely unexpressed but almost universally understood. It's as if all golfers take a form of the Hippocratic oath—"Do no harm." Notice next time you play how experienced golfers keep the course in good shape, don't interfere with other players, and avoid doing anything that would make the game less enjoyable for anyone.

As a group, golfers are the best sportsmen and sportswomen there are.

This Special Game

Those who fish have a special awareness of the sunrise, when a still lake reflects the browns and greens of the surrounding trees, when the damp cool air raises goose bumps on the arms, and when only the chirps of nearby birds break the silence. Mountain climbers know the desperate fatigue of accomplishment and the 100-mile vistas from the summit. Scuba divers enjoy nose-to-nose delights of flashing fin and sometimes heart-stopping fear as a large dark shadow passes slowly overhead.

Because a golf course is what it is, golfers know all these things and much more. Simply being outdoors is part of it. Depending on the course, you are in forest, glade, park, or desert; on a river walkway, urban trail, or sandy shoreline. Golf is a walk in the park, a climb up a hill, and a stroll along a pond. Weather is always a factor. Blue skies and warm temperatures are the favorite, but playing in strong winds adds flavor, as does racing darkness to finish a quick nine. Rain is almost universally decried. But in what other game can you chase a rainbow as you play?

No other game offers the variety of golf. Henry Longhurst observes:

> Every other game is played on the same kind of pitch the world over. One football field is like another; one cricket pitch like the next, except that in one case the background may be the village chestnuts and in another the gasometers. Yet not only is every golfing pitch different from all others, but it consists

of 18 little pitches within itself. Thus an almost inexhaustible supply of golfing problems presents itself.

All courses present problems; the best ones do so beautifully. Topping many lists are Pine Valley, Cypress Point, Pebble Beach, and Augusta National in the United States; Portmarnock, St. Andrews, and Royal Dornoch in the British Isles; Royal Melbourne and New South Wales in Australia; Hirono in Japan; and the Gavea Golf Club in Brazil. Every couple of years *Golf Digest* magazine lists 100 of the best courses in the U.S. and could easily double that number without lowing its standards much. Worldwide there must be 5,000 wonderful places to play out of an estimated 30,000 courses.

There are oddities. A least half a dozen courses are within racetracks, so if you lose with horses, you may later win with birdies (sorry). La Paz Country Club sits 12,000 feet high in Bolivia, so everyone can be a big hitter. There is at least one par-7 hole in the world—a 948-yard hole at Kooian Island Golf Course in Australia—and one course over 8,000 yards long, the International Golf Club in Bolton, Massachusetts, which weighs in at 8,325 yards and boasts a par-6 fifth hole at 715 yards. Not too far away, just outside Washington, D.C., is the longest hole in the United States, the par-6 12th hole at Meadow Farms Golf Course—841 yards from the blue tees.

For sheer golfing pleasure nothing beats a tough, beautiful hole. One of the best is Foxy, the 14th at Royal Dornoch. Lying on the far northeastern coast of Scotland, Dornoch is off the path of most golfing tourists. But you should take a look at the course on the advice of highly respected golf writer Herbert Warren Wind, who says, "No golfer has completed his education unless he's played and studied Royal Dornoch." It was the birthplace of designer Donald Ross; the course, although golf had been played there for centuries, was formally laid out by Old Tom Morris. Unlike most links, where the run-up shot is the preferred technique, here it is almost impossible. The greens sit on mounds with steep banks; add sand ridges, gorse, heather, rough, hollows, and wind, and Dornoch provides all the challenge you could want. Tom Watson once played 54 holes in 24 hours here and declared it was the most fun he'd ever had playing golf.

The course starts simply enough with a short, straightaway par-4 of 331 yards. This is followed by a reasonable par-3 of 177 yards and the first of many raised greens. The second is guarded by a bunker on each side and a mound in front of the green to steer short balls into the sand. After the second, though, it seems that each hole demands more than the prior one. By the time you reach the 14th you've endured one hole where the fairway is 40 feet below the tee, fairway mounds of 7 to 10 feet covered with rough grass, falls of 12 feet from the greens' surfaces, another landing area 50 feet below the level of the initial fairway, dozens of deep greenside bunkers, and, it seems, always playing into the wind.

Foxy is a long 454-yard par-4. From the tee the fairway looks like a straightaway: not a bunker anywhere and no water. A closer look reveals a fundamental flaw—the hole has no green. On the left side of the fairway are grassy mounds. On the right are rows of grass-covered hills as big as locomotives. At the far end of the fairway is more golf course. But no green. Finally, after much searching, you'll spot it hiding behind one of the right-side hills of buried freight trains. It's another raised green.

Trouble begins at the tee. Pull the ball into the left-hand mounds and there is no shot to the green. Push or slice into the series of buried trains, ditto. Assuming you hit the ball with your absolute best Sunday drive, you're still 200 to 220 yards from the flagstick. And the raised green you've finally discovered sits obliquely to the fairway. With a wood or long iron in your hand, you're looking at a steep bank of 5 feet on the left of the green and 10 feet on the right. Once you've chipped on (you won't be on the green with your second), the surface is rolling and fast. A five here is a very good score, and a six nothing to be ashamed of. And just to balance things out, all those downhill tee shots you had earlier are made up in one hole at the 16th (High hole), where it appears as if the landing area for your drive is at the base of a cliff 1,000 feet high.

But as much as tough par-4s make golf interesting, there are other ways. Short holes add spice to a round, at times as eye-opening as biting into a jalapeño. At "one-shot" holes, you have little opportunity to make up for a bad tee shot. A few take maximum advantage of this all-or-nothing element: the 16th at Cypress Point, 230 yards over the rocky Pacific shoreline; the 12th at Augusta National, a narrow green with a pond in front and swirling winds above; and the island 17th at the Tournament Players Club in Ponte Vedra.

A terrific one-shot hole deserving a quick look is another one in Scotland and much copied elsewhere. The Redan hole at North Berwick is a 200-yard par-3 distinguished by a large, deep bunker guarding the left part of the green with a significant tilt of the putting surface from left to right. You're faced with either flying over the bunker or shaping the shot, depending on the placement of the pin. Wind also plays an important part in your choice of approach. Do you hold a draw against the wind or ride the breeze with a fade? Choosing correctly but hitting too long, too short, or with too much curve usually leaves a challenging second shot—often with another decision about lofting or bumping toward the hole. Island greens, which require only a high shot of the correct distance, offer only black-and-white definitions of success.

The ideal golf hole, architect MacKenzie Ross believes, "puts a question mark into the player's mind when he arrives on the tee to play it." Many players will criticize a hole before taking the time to understand its demands. If you play the 16th at St. Andrews (or any of the other Old Course holes, for that matter), you'll easily understand the concept. No less than Alister MacKenzie noted that 16 was a weak hole and would be much improved if the Deacon Syme bunker were moved to the left to allow longer hitters a chance to aim at a slightly larger target between the bunkers and what was then the railroad tracks. Ted Blackwell, a long-ball hitter at the turn of the 20th century, replied, "Then you would move it to the spot which I think is ideal for placing my drive."

It took him 35 years, Blackwell said, to discover a small hollow to the left of the Principal's Nose bunker. From there he could run up his second to the green and avoid most of the trouble coming into play from everywhere else on the fairway.

Thirty-five years might seem like a long time to spend figuring out how to play a golf hole, but that's why we play. Surely this is the game of a lifetime.

2

THINKING ABOUT GOLF

Ownership

If you owned the copyright to golf, along with all the equipment and all the courses around the world, how would you manage the development of this great game of yours?

If you ran it strictly as a business, you'd want demand to grow and customer satisfaction to be high. One way to do this would be to meet the expectations of new players. Provide what the customers want, making sure what they want is what you can provide and vice versa. You'd want standardization, predictability, and profitability, just like those fast-food and lube-shop chains.

If you owned the game and thought of it as a legacy, on the other hand, you'd do all you could to minimize damage to the courses, maybe require a license to play (as is done in some places), and keep the highest standards as the norm. No one would be allowed to play unless he knew what he was doing and didn't detract from the pleasure of other players. Bad behavior would warrant immediate expulsion. Conditions would be impeccable, with tee times at a minimum of 12-minute intervals. The staff would be courteous and helpful, the clubhouse warm and inviting.

Reality, of course, is somewhere in the middle. No one person can control the game, and at most courses anyone with the price of a green fee can tee up. Ownership has to be an attitude within the player—a beneficent attitude, we hope, and as widespread a beneficent attitude as we can make it.

We are all owners of the game when we stand on the first tee, swing at the ball, or even put on our shoes in the parking lot or relax at the 19th hole. Do you act like an owner? Are you investing in your property? Are you keeping your children's inheritance safe and secure?

You are if you play by the rules and observe course etiquette. At the risk of preaching to the choir, it may be that the only way to retain golf's special qualities is to emphasize playing by the rules and observing the old-fashioned niceties. Any game can be played in any way. Kids invent variations all the time. The evolution of golf attests to the effects of development, both good and bad.

Some rules become absurd as styles and technology change. Dan Jenkins wrote about a woman with gold-plated arteries who was denied entry into the dining room of the Cypress Point Club by a huffy maître d'. Her crime? She was wearing a designer pant suit instead of the required skirt or dress. Without a fuss, she left the entryway and returned after a moment without the offending pants. Instead, she wore her raincoat wrapped around her waist. "That will do nicely," the maître d' said, nose still high in the air.* Discrimination of any kind in golf—whether based on clothing, sex, color, religion, age, ability, or culture—needs close scrutiny to determine if it's enhancing the game (as when faster players are given the early tee times) or being used to disenfranchise. Standards are important, but they must benefit both the individual and the game.

If you owned the game, what kind of owner would you be?

---

*Hall of Fame golfer Patty Sheehan had this bumper sticker on her car from another perspective: WOMEN WHO SEEK EQUALITY WITH MEN LACK AMBITION.

An English Club

If you happened to live a little south of Blackpool on the west coast of England not long before the turn of the 20th century, you might have been asked to join a newly formed club situated in the sandy dunes of St. Anne's. A letter to the local gentry was sent out on February 23, 1886, by J. T. and J. S. Fair, proposing the formation of a club and the creation of a golf course on the old Clifton estate. The first competition was held two months later (they designed and built courses faster in the old days) and was won by 25-handicapper J. Mugliston with a solid 123. Finishing last was W. P. Fullagar at 244. Only two of the competitors had played more than the few days the course had been open. Although new, the club developed strict handicap rules. An experiment was tried after a couple of years in which the maximum handicap was increased to 60, perhaps to attract new members. However, when John Allen posted a 127 less 60 for a net score of 67, the handicap maximum was quickly reduced to 30 and Mr. Allen's handicap reduced from 60 to scratch!

By 1900 a new links and clubhouse greeted members. It was the beginning of the golden age. The steward at St. Andrews was lured away and the bar was well stocked with fine old whiskey, fine old Glenlivet, fine old Highland malt, Devonshire sloe gin, Hennessy brandy, and Upman's Concha Fina and Yuclan's Eligante cigars. Two dozen copper spittoons were purchased, as were playing cards, dominoes, a chess game, and of course tables for billiards and pool. Women and men played different courses, and the clubhouse was designed with separate entrances for the disparate sexes.* Yet for all this organization, the club retained a homey feel. A letter sent to members read: "If you are coming to the Autumn Meeting, Mr. Bowman would feel greatly obliged if you would contribute a song or two at the smoking concert."

In 1926 King George V anointed the club the "Royal Lytham and St. Anne's Golf Club." That same year it hosted its first Open championship. Walter Hagen, Tommy Armour, and Bob Jones led the American entrants. It was here that Jones forgot his contestant's badge and was refused entry. He politely walked to the spectator's entrance, paid his two shillings and sixpence entry (first time a fee was charged at the Open), and made his way to the tee. Jones won, two strokes ahead of Hagen and Al Waltrous. Later that year he went on to win the U.S. Open at Scioto.

The depression of the late 1920s and much of the 1930s reduced the club's membership to 398 and put its finances into an awful state. If you joined during this time, you played with the chairman of the Handicap Committee and two other officials. Your handicap was determined not by your score, but by their impression of your ball-striking ability.

Bob Jones returned during World War II to play a match to raise funds for the Red Cross. Many American fliers stationed nearby played the course during the long summer evenings. If you waited until 1948 to join the club, you were in luck: Entrance fees were abolished to encourage membership. A new club tie, not necessarily superseding the old one, was designed in 1954. It was also decided that the council would return to meeting first, then having dinner and drinks afterward, because the reverse arrangement tended to lead to more heated discussions.

If you were a member in the 1960s, you might have voted for the proposal to gain ownership of the land. Squire

*In 1913 boys were assigned two-hour shifts to protect the greens from rampaging Suffragettes.

Harry Clifton offered to sell the property for £50,000. This was when the original lease of £100 per year still had 30 years left. Members, comparing the cost of buying against a mere £100-per-year lease, voted 58 to 23 against the purchase. Just a few years later that same £50,000 wouldn't buy a three-bedroom house, and certainly it will nevermore touch the price of the 147 acres offered at that amount. The new owner, Guardian Assurance, did renegotiate a new lease for £1,000 a year for 60 years. Long enough for current members to enjoy the club, but a sad fate given what could have been.

If you were a member today, you would look back at a wonderful tournament history. The club has hosted many national amateur championships, the Ryder Cup, and, most important, a number of British Opens. Open winners have included Jones, Locke, Charles, Jacklin, Ballesteros, and Lehman. The Jacklin Open of 1969 was chronicled by the *L.A. Times* writer Jim Murray, who described the course and the deep grass this way: "There are places here you could hit your ball, where they might have trouble finding you. You not only have trouble hitting a green, you have trouble finding it. The fairways are really unfair-ways, although there is room for two comfortably. At first glance it looks like an empty lot from Cleveland."

Next time you watch the British Open at Lytham and St. Anne's, think a little about its history—and how the golf course may not exist after the current lease expires. And play it if you can; the hospitality is legendary. Is that the sound of bulldozers in the distance?

Golf's Unfortunate Side

Private clubs have long been a bastion of discrimination—that's why they're formed. People like to create an external home and invite friends over for mutual enjoyment. As long as they abide by laws and regulations, clubs should be allowed to have as members anyone they please. The American Constitution's First Amendment defines the right of freedom of association. As our society grows up, it is assumed that the clubs to belong to will have as members the most interesting mix possible. Those that discriminate by physical features will house rigid thinkers who seek and appreciate only those who think similarly or not at all, which is pretty much the same thing. Golf cannot be proud of all of its history and some of its present-day behavior.*

Imagine the rivalry if Tiger Woods had been a contemporary of Jack Nicklaus; if both arrived on the tour in 1962 as Jack did. Fat Jack against the Skinny Kid, and both trying to knock Arnie off the throne. One would boom a drive down the fairway, then the other would launch another rocket. In 1962 the fireworks could have happened. In 1961 they could not. "Caucasian Race only," the rules read at that time.

---

*Exclusion/inclusion can get crazy. The 1999 National Minority College Golf Championship (talk about exclusionary) ruled the team from Texas Pan American ineligible. The team from Bethune-Cookman won. Guess which team fielded Mexican Americans and which had white guys.

The change came thanks in part to boxing champion Joe Lewis, who insisted that some of his "colored" golf professional friends be allowed to play in some California tournaments, but more to the passionate efforts of nongolfer Stanley Mosk. In 1960 Mosk, as California Attorney General, put the PGA on notice that because of its discriminatory policy, it would not be allowed to compete over any public course in California. He also alerted other states' attorneys general and suggested they do likewise. To its shame, the PGA resisted in any number of ways, but finally gave in to the pressure, not necessarily to do what was right. In November 1961 civil rights became part of the tour, and in 1964 Pete Brown at the Waco Turner Open became the first African American to win an official PGA Tour event.

Race has long been an issue in golf, and so has gender. Mentioned earlier were the experiences women had at some of the early British clubs. The same kind of attitudes exist today. Women are suing private clubs all over the place to gain playing and other rights equal to those of male members. A Boston-area club was told to compensate nine female golfers $2 million for years of bad tee times and other acts of discrimination. Women, of course, have had to endure less-than-stellar male behavior in places other than the golf course. But boorishness and exclusion are only part of the discrimination mix. Women's tees are often an afterthought and usually don't allow them approach shots with the same clubs as men, making the game both intimidating and more difficult for women. However, as more girls take up sports and more golf courses run programs to make women feel more welcome, this problem should eventually become one of golf's long-past growing pains.

Golf is going to do the right thing. All races will play. Women will have rights equal to men. Clubs will have freedom to accept whoever they please as members. Society will continue to mature.

So as we're getting things straightened out, what about carts for the disabled on the tour? Golf is one of the few professional sports that could encompass such aids. Should more people have a chance to compete at the highest level?

Casey Martin won the right to use a cart on the PGA Tour through a 1998 court decision and an appeal. On the one hand, it's a victory for the individual, for the disabled, and for the game that prides itself on its newfound sense of equality. On the other hand, the right to use a cart is a blow to courses that may have to be revamped to accommodate all players, another nail in the coffin of a game that used to be natural, and a concern to all those who want athleticism and fitness to be a part of high-level competition. And in a small way it is another blow to those who want golfers' scores to be achieved unaided. The use of caddies to help players line up was one thump to these values, as is the slow but sure move to lessen the player's personal responsibility for scorekeeping and knowing the rules. Many decry the penalties suffered by professionals when a rule is broken. Most recently PGA Tour player Brian Gay during the Honda Classic waited for his still-moving putt to drop; when it did, he thought he had tied for the lead. Unfortunately, he waited about 13 seconds and not the 10 allowed, and suffered a one-stroke penalty. What else could the ruling have been?

Casey Martin is only the tip of the iceberg of a movement to make the game fit the needs, expectations, even dreams of the individual, rather than the other way around. But perhaps the horse has already left the barn. Many courses require the use of riding carts. Professionals and others use yardage books with laser-measured distances accurate to within inches. Sixty-degree wedges make a mockery of greenside trouble. Golf balls can be chosen for their spin to within 100 rpm. Nobody hits a 2-iron anymore. When individuals and special-interest groups push the envelope, the spirit of the game may be the loser.

R-E-S-P-E-C-T

Golf often becomes a lifelong love affair. It can begin with fascination fueled by curiosity or with the same reluctance and uncertainty as a blind date. Whatever the introduction, there is a long period of adjustment, learning golf's wiles and whims and experiencing every human emotion. Some beginners get bored, some get frustrated, some quit, and many fall in love. But as in any relationship, elements can become tarnished, made common or too familiar; which breeds disrespect, disdain, and finally disinterest. Relationships require investment. Few of today's new players are willing to put forth the effort. They expect the game to be easy, fun, a five-hour fantasy of hitting the ball a mile in a Disney-like setting. Frustration is a downer. A bad bounce is unacceptable, a lost ball unforgivable. The challenge that enriched so many players seems to be going the way of the dodo bird. Few these days play the ball "down." Few golfers play by the rules. Few fix ball marks in the green, and many don't bother with divots. New players want it their way. The old standards have become old-fashioned.

It's a shame when one jet-age professional golfer proclaims the British Open "inconvenient." It's distressing when others bemoan the conditions of the greens, crucify their pro-am partners, or berate the people who volunteered many hours to make their community's once-a-year tournament a success. Tom Weiskopf is an unfortunate contemporary example after his display of immaturity in the 1996 Senior Open. There, using more swear words than a bosun's mate, he berated Senior amateur champion Jim Stahl, his playing competitor during the first two rounds, complaining of everything from the pace of play to the size of ball markers. Volatile Tom demonstrated how a good player doesn't necessarily do what's good for golf. Then again, a few members of the U.S. Ryder Cup team at The Country Club in Brookline in 1999 caused quite a stir. Justin Leonard sank a long putt on the 17th hole of his match with Josè Maria Olazabal. American players and wives dashed onto the green in celebration. Olazabal still had a putt, a shorter one, to render Leonard's moot. Comments about the outburst ranged from "it was spontaneous, how can you blame them for celebrating" to Olazabal's own "[it was an] ugly picture." Unfortunately, this incident is only one milestone on a superhighway of boorish acts. The PGA Tour stop in Phoenix is notorious for rude and other boozed-up behavior. David Duval recently heard chants of "hit it in the water" on the 13th. Others are booed if they appear to be laying up on the drivable par-4 17th. At the 1997 U.S. Open at Congressional Davis Love commented, "It's becoming more like a baseball game or a basketball game where people think they can yell or say anything they want." Most golfers think we can, and should, do better.

Golf must remain a game to be loved, the player knowing without doubt that he is better for playing it, and that there isn't a more enjoyable challenge on the face of the earth.

Other sports and pastimes boast more athleticism, endurance, power, and need for quick reflexes, but they also suffer significant problems. A recent television video program highlighted a high school football game where the quarterback took the hike and pretended that the wrong ball was in play. Holding the ball over his head, he strolled through the confused opposition toward the sidelines, where a coach held up what seemed to be the correct game ball. As soon as the quarterback was clear of the other team's players, he dashed down the sideline for a touchdown. Evidently this trick play had been taught by the coaches. Another television program showed the home video of a Little League baseball game marked by parents attacking the umpire and then one another. Twenty-three policemen were sent to the scene to quell the growing riot. One high school wrestler head-butted an official into unconsciousness. At the professional level, basketball coaches are strangled by players and baseball umpires are spit upon. So far golf is different.

In a national survey of golfers, over 90 percent of respondents believed that sports can help build character, and most believed golf did it differently than other sports, largely because of its emphasis on honor.

But golf is changing. It is always changing, but now it may be moving in a direction that will destroy some of it while rendering what's left a shadow of the grand game.

Frank Thomas, technical director of the USGA, said, "Golf is a dynamic game that must change with the times," at the 1996 Theory in Practice Conference in Coleraine, Ireland. This international meeting, held every four years, alternates with the World Scientific Congress of Golf in St. Andrews. These gatherings attract hundreds of engineers, physicists, agronomists, ergonomists, chemists, and technicians. High-handicaps in white lab coats put their heads together in dozens of meeting rooms. The goal: to figure out how to get the ball into the hole easier, quicker, cheaper, and with less wear and tear on player and course. Science, new players, and businesses are ganging up on the traditions.

The new generation has been raised on continuous quality improvement. The question on everybody's mind is: How can we make it better? Let's change the dimple pattern on balls to enhance aerodynamics. Let's offer a wider array of shaft types, flex, kickpoints, and weights. Fifty new models of clubs are introduced every year. A classy course must have railroad ties, or double greens, or split fairways, or something. New ideas and new products must be found. Greens in fruit shapes might be the favored marketing enticement for this year. Next year it will be different-colored ones. Who knows what inventions are over the horizon? Technology, including golf technology, is developing faster than our sense of what is right.

If the ads are to be believed, titanium clubs will increase driver distance up to 40 yards. A ball that matches your clubs, swing, and personality can fly higher, roll smoother, and stop faster. Soft spikes can shave off a couple of stokes by protecting today's smoother greens, while special putter inserts help you feel the ball into the hole. Custom-fitted clubs will keep your ball on the fairway and help you reach greens from farther away. Heck, choose equipment carefully and you can end your shopping day a plus-2-handicap.

The hype is aimed at improving scores, and indeed scores are important. You win or lose, you track progress, you define success by noting what you shot. The score is not significant, however. You as a golfer are much more than a number in a little box on the right-hand side of a rectangular piece of heavy paper. This concept, too, is being buried in the avalanche of powerful forces.

By consumer demand and commercial response, golf is being diluted; made easy and comfortable for more players. Individual effort is minimized. We ride in carts driven down concrete roadways and carry three or four computer-designed clubs to the nearest sprinkler head that is marked with yardage to the front, the middle, and the back of the green. Prestige resorts employ tastefully attired forecaddies to rake the bunkers and jog ahead, minimizing delays and all but eliminating lost balls. These places groom the tee boxes into flower gardens, polish the greens marble smooth, and clip every blemish from flora and fauna. Golf has become artificial. The sweet sting has been taken out of the game. An afternoon of golf is as exciting as wading ankle-deep in a kiddie pool. The magical connection with the earth that has made golf special for so long is fading into designer pink and asphalt black, perhaps to be lost.

This new generation wants golf to be like fast food: predictable, available, easy, and completely comprehensible. Just where all those scientists are headed. Business is involved, too. Golf courses are designed to appeal to specific markets: high-end tracks designed by big-name players, resorts with fairway mounds that bounce balls back toward the middle, and monster layouts that attract masochists willing to spend $200 and more for a lifetime of stories. Greens float in the middle of lakes, approachable only by boat. Eight different tees are strewn at the beginning of each hole to assure maximum golfing pleasure. It's as if golf isn't good enough as it was, but must be improved. The *Mona Lisa* is old and pretty good as is, but today anyone can digitize her and enhance her eyes, smile, or bust line. The same kind of thing may be happening to golf.

Rules

Strict rules define the essence of golf. Take the position of Bob Jones after he was praised for calling a penalty on himself 70 years ago. "There is only one way to play the game," he said. "You might as well praise a man for not robbing a bank."

For nongolfers and new golfers, golf's rules and etiquette make the game at best a mystery and at worst irritating and exclusionary. Everything possible should be done to help new golfers accept and enjoy this part of the game. Here's how you can do this.

Know the rules and follow the rules. Hardly anyone does, but following the rules provides wonderful structure. And they're not that hard to understand—at least not the ones necessary for normal play. However, you might want to:

- Buy a few rulebooks each year from the USGA (or the R&A), read one, store one in your bag and play by what it says, and maybe have an extra somewhere to give away. Quietly going about your business provides a strong example for others, but to demand that everyone do as you do is counterproductive. Ron Monaco of Seattle, a low-handicap golfer, once played in a club tournament where he had to give his opponent 29 strokes. His opponent didn't know or play by the rules. Ron corrected the man here and there—never imposing a penalty, but educating along the way—and won an exciting and fulfilling match on the 18th. Both men enjoyed the competition, the companionship, and the elements of the game that one taught and the other learned.

- Play the ball as you find it unless doing so is obnoxious or clearly not in the best interest of course upkeep or fair play.

- When taking a drop, don't just flip the ball to the ground. Drop it correctly. This is a simple yet clear way of showing that the rules are important.

- Post all your scores. This provides a good example for others, who will notice that you include every game, good and bad. And it also provides a healthy degree of self-satisfaction that doesn't ooze into self-righteousness.

- Call penalties on yourself as needed. Let your opponents know as soon as you do. If done right, this is one of the best ways to demonstrate and enhance golf values.

- Call them flagsticks, bunkers, hazards, fellow competitors, playing partners, or playing companions. Knowing the correct name, and using it, is one of the early steps toward understanding.

- Know that the ball moves only if it changes places, not wobbles. Knowing this and the following tidbits is another way of understanding and promoting good golf:

1. *Through the green* means the whole course except the putting green and teeing ground of the hole being played, and all hazards.
2. There is no minimum distance the hole must be from the edge of the green.
3. The flag is pulled by the one lying closest to the hole, then replaced by the one first in.
4. The person farthest from the hole plays next; being on or off the green doesn't matter.
5. A ball is in bounds if any part of it is in bounds. The same is true with water hazards. You can play a ball moving in a water hazard if you do so without undue delay (such as waiting for it to get closer to the green).
6. When relief is taken, full relief must be taken.

7. You have 10 seconds for a ball on the lip to fall into the hole.
8. For the most part, you can only lift and clean your ball if it's on the green—not if you're identifying it, not if you're moving it out of someone's way, and not to see if it's damaged.
9. The player is "dormie" if he's ahead the same number of holes as there are left to play.

- Be polite. Nothing differentiates golf from other activities better than politeness. There are many ways to do this:

  1. Do nothing that will adversely affect anyone else.
  2. Play at a reasonable pace.
  3. Let faster groups through, even someone playing alone, and especially when it's late and you're trying to finish before dark. It's true that a single has no standing on the course, because anyone playing alone is not in a match. But it's likely that a single is out there working on shots or just enjoying a few late holes. Let him play through.
  4. Make sure the course is in better shape after you played than before.
  5. Don't bring a cell phone. If you're that important, stay where you're needed.
  6. Play so that you hardly ever have to shout "fore."
  7. Play ready golf, and be ready.

- When searching for a lost ball, don't wander around the area randomly crisscrossing each other's lines of search. Make a best estimate of where the ball landed, subtract 10 to 20 yards, then all move in a line toward the hole.
- Wear soft spikes whenever possible. Fix marks on the green when you're walking to your ball, waiting your turn, or finished putting.
- Walk the course.

- Know the local practice of replacing divots or filling the gouge with sand instead.
- Respect the needs of the professional staff and grounds crew.

If you owned the course, isn't all this what you'd want? Nobody can control everything, but maybe a few thoughtful players can influence things here and there. A whole bunch of folks might just nudge everyone else in the right direction.

A Fair Game

It is the nature of our game to reward us for trying, but not necessarily for the quality of the effort. Holes-in-one have been made after a ball rebounded off trees, carts, bunker rakes, wild deer, and sleeping spaniels. It may be part of the charm of golf that we succeed sometimes simply because we're out playing the game. At the same time, it's the nature of golf to withhold reward from—or even punish—good shots. A beautiful tee shot, long and down the middle, can be deflected by a sprinkler head into the rough or, worse, into a pond or out of bounds. A perfect 20-foot putt, mere inches from falling into the cup, can be deflected by an old spike mark. The rules can conspire against us. Popular tour golfer Kel Nagle played well in the second round of a tournament, but his marker mistakenly entered Kel's nine-hole score in the space for the ninth-hole score. Instead of signing for a 35 on the nine, Kel (according to the rules holding a player responsible for his score) had to accept shooting 35 on the ninth hole and 105 for the round. Worse, Roberto deVicenzo lost his chance to win the Masters when his playing companion, Tommy Aaron, accidentally recorded a four instead of the three deVincenzo actually scored on the 17th during the final round. All the world knew he shot 65 to tie Bob Golby, but the rules recognized only the 66 he signed for.*

---

*The women's tour has not been immune. Jackie Pung won the 1957 Women's Open with a final-round 72. However, she was disqualified when it was noted she signed for a five rather than a six on the fourth hole. Jackie's total was correct, but Betsy Rawls took the title.

It seems unfair that a 1-foot putt counts the same as a 250-yard drive, and that a ball 1 inch out of bounds results in a penalty stroke and loss of distance, too. It's unfair that a ball hit 1 foot too short can fall into a bunker, and a ball can hit the flagstick and rebound into a stream. It's unfair that your opponent can hit a slice that bounces off a tree into the fairway, while you hit a perfect tee shot that ends up in someone's divot.

What is *fair*, anyway? A dictionary says the word means "impartial" or "according to the rules." When people say that golf is unfair, what they are describing is a child's idea of fairness—that good things will happen if you try hard. This misses the point. Golf fits every definition of *fairness* in the dictionary if you define the term from the game's point of view and not the player's. The rules are as clear as human thought can make them, and they're critically evaluated continually and changed as needed. The course sits and waits, visible to the eyes and further defined by pars, ratings, yardage, and slope. Natural elements like wind and sun are as unbiased as anything can be. The ball goes where you hit it and waits until you're ready to hit it again. Nothing could be fairer than golf—except in its choice of adversaries. Golf seems to be an unfair game because it pits you against yourself; an impossibly difficult opponent.

Life Is a Metaphor for Golf

We were discussing life around the water cooler one morning when someone said, "You know, life is a metaphor for golf." We quickly informed him he had it backward. "No," he insisted, "that's how I heard it."

We danced around the idea until we were dizzy, so a small group of us journeyed at lunchtime to the Half Staff Café where our local oracle Angus McIrons hangs out. Angus is the typical Fife-born former caddie-player turned guru; cigarette-stained fingers, burr as thick as a tweed coat, deep lines etched in a ruddy face, and a handicap of plus-3 despite being over 100 years old.

"Aye," he nodded, "'tis a metaphor, as they say, but no hoo ye ken. The metaphor lies within, no withoot." He then dismissed us by turning back to continue sweet-talking Jennifer the bartender.

Back at the office we were deep in debate about golf and life when Tommy from the mailroom walked by. "I believe Kipling's thoughts as carved over the entrance to Wimbledon's center court are germane here: 'Meeting triumph and disaster and treating those two impostors just the same.'" We soon chased him out of there.

By quitting time we thought we had it figured out, and we had to give old Angus and young Tommy their due. The metaphor is indeed within the player. A true golfer who has taken a mulligan on the first tee senses that what he plays thereafter is no longer golf. Life is a metaphor for golf. That is, golf can, and should, be played like life. An action in life is irrevocable, just as every golf stroke can be. Anyone who has refused a mulligan, counts all the strokes no matter how many, and calls a self-imposed penalty knows the satisfaction of playing the game as it should be—accepting the outcome of a best effort and moving on.

At first acknowledging a whiff or self-assessing a penalty occurs only after convoluted internal debate. Later it gets easier, approaching automatic. This internal psychodrama is the real metaphor.

By accepting the inherent and sometimes cruel realities of life and of golf, you do much more than learn to play by the rules and be a good sport. You create and sustain an important core value: honor.

Life and golf as intertwining metaphors teach that the victory is in the effort—never in the result. That's why golf is the only game whose participants are genuinely able to wish their opponents well. We are all competing for the same thing, and we can all win the game even if it's against each other.

Golf is a metaphor because it demands our best and promises nothing in return, and because if we give it our best we are rewarded no matter what the outcome. Life is the same way.

Three-time U.S. Open champion Hale Irwin suggests that "a man's [golf] performance is the outward manifestation of who, in his heart, he really thinks he is."

However, golf can be like an open vault door in an empty bank, offering self-demeaning opportunity with each new shot. Although cheating is the worst crime that can be committed in golf, golfers are human and not immune to temptation, especially regarding what are considered minor infractions of the rules. Many Sunday players roll the ball to a supportive tuft of grass without concern. Some replace the ball on the green carelessly, but make sure it's to the side of an unrepaired ball mark. What are these players saying about what's inside their hearts then? They need to learn that it's okay not to be up to the challenge, but to try anyway. "The game embarrasses you until you feel inadequate and pathetic," Ben Crenshaw says. "You want to cry like a child."

"Good golf isn't a matter of hitting great shots," adds Lee Trevino. "It's finding a way to make your bad ones not so bad." Most golfers don't know this. They think a bad shot is a reflection of personal weakness. This sense of inadequacy, coupled with relative ignorance of the rules, makes experiencing honor while playing golf impossible.

One of the sports highlights of the year is the Superbowl, pitting the two best teams from the American and National Football Leagues. One game for everything. Imagine an exhausting battle late in the fourth quarter. The game is close, one team ahead by 4 but the other team driving toward the goal line. With only seconds left in the game, the quarterback desperately heaves the ball into the end zone. The receiver makes a diving catch. The referee signals a touchdown. The crowd goes wild.

Except the receiver runs to the referee, holding the ball out, shaking his head. He tells the official he didn't catch it. The ball hit the ground as he was diving for it. No touchdown. His team loses. Can you imagine this happening? Probably not. In our society winning is more important than honor. The truth takes second place. But it happens in golf.

You have just caused a penalty stroke, called it on yourself, and thus lost the hole—and you feel a weird sense of satisfaction. That's why golf will drive you crazy and why you will enjoy the trip so much.

Once you know and play by the rules, and define an error as only something to improve upon, honor then becomes part of the game and part of you.

Isn't golf, and aren't golfers, amazing?

Beyond the Boundaries
of the Course

If golf can develop a sense of honor and people of good character, it's a simple matter to conclude that golfers, when mobilized either as individuals or in groups, can significantly contribute to the well-being of others. Golf fans are well aware of the millions of dollars raised by the professional tours for local charities. This, however, reflects only the relative affluence of many golfers. A better indication of the trend is the First Tee movement. This effort, supported initially by the USGA, Augusta National Golf Club, PGA Tour, and PGA of America, has the mission of providing golfing experiences to those who would otherwise be left out, mostly inner-city minorities. If done correctly—which means including golf's core values along with swinging and playing instruction—this is a wonderful first step.

However, three elements remain to be included:

- Presenting the core values in effective ways.
- Creating long-term connections to golf so early frustrations don't lead to quitting.
- Ensuring that the have-nots have enough opportunity over a long period of time to connect with the haves.

The last element is probably most critical. Yes, it helps to have the young and poor play against each other on an inner-city nine-hole course. But we can do much better. Lewis V. Horne Jr., former president of the National Minority Golf Association, puts the idea this way:

> In the end, instead of being a bastion of elitism and privilege, golf could evolve into a pursuit that affords opportunities for all people to not only benefit from the individualistic attributes of golf—positive values, behavioral standards and role models—but also to associate themselves with other segments of society that they might not otherwise encounter.

Certainly our efforts would not be in vain.

We have to assume more responsibility. Delightful responsibility, really. To ourselves, the game we love, our society, and the world. Golf can and should enhance the individual and the world.

A few businesses have provided wonderful examples of the importance and effect of golf values extended beyond the boundaries of the course. Moe Norman, the eccentric but talented Canadian golf professional, never enjoyed much financial success. His personality severely restricted his ability to benefit from his dedication to golf and his superb ball striking. When the Titleist company learned that Moe was struggling, it immediately provided him with a handsome monthly stipend for life.

Although not needy like Moe Norman, Gene Sarazen was offered and accepted 38 consecutive two-year contracts with the Wilson Sporting Goods company. He was paid not for his golfing ability, but for his value as a gentlemanly spokesman.

The Sara Lee Corporation also did right by golf. For 12 years Sara Lee sponsored the LPGA tournament in Nashville, Tennessee. In addition to awarding the winner first-place prize money, the company also gave her a diamond and emerald necklace, a one-of-a-kind Gibson guitar, and, for the next year, a small gift in her locker whenever she played an LPGA tournament. Even nonwinners were remembered on special occasions. It wasn't the gift, it was the thought. The world needs more of what golf can offer.

3

THE GOLF TRADE

Change Is Constant

In the 1890s mechanical hammers began replacing the strong arms of club makers, and irons became cheaper and more uniform. (This shift from handmade to machine-made clubs is interesting in the light of today's "custom-fit" movement—found in Henry Griffiths' and Zevo clubs, to name just two.) Hickory, the preferred shaft material, was often hand-sanded during this period in an attempt to match the swing characteristics among a player's clubs. Also during this time, the Haskell ball came on the scene, and iron clubs were made with grooves and other scoring. Prior to this most clubs had smooth faces.

During the first 20-odd years of the 20th century, the golf ball saw considerable change. Balata covers replaced gutta-percha, dimples replaced bumps, and the official size was adjusted half a dozen times. Steel shafts became legal and step-down steel shafts were invented; these shafts allowed truly matched sets of clubs. In the 1930s, clubs were limited to 14 and Gene Sarazen invented the sand wedge. The 1940s brought laminated woods and the USGA's Initial Velocity Standard in order to gain control over golf-ball development.

The second half of the century saw fiberglass shafts in the 1950s and aluminum 10 years later. Also during the 1960s, cast clubs appeared, along with one-piece and two-piece balls. In the 1970s it was more dimples, different dimples, and different dimple arrangements. If the ball wasn't allowed to go faster, then the flight characteristics would have to be improved. In the 1980s the USGA was compelled to initiate the Symmetry Standard so that ball flight could not be easily bought. Metal woods first appeared in the 1980s, too, and in the 1990s were everywhere.

As of this writing, titanium is the big story, in both clubs and balls. See your newspaper for the latest details, because change is constant and everywhere. Golf equipment has gone through many alterations over the years, some long lasting, others only failed experiments. The game's tools are always changing. Knowing what's good and what's not so good shouldn't take the mind of a rocket scientist.

Or perhaps your mind is more like Terry Koehler, president of Reid Lockhart, a maker of old-fashioned clubs (blade irons and persimmon woods):

> People are getting a little disgruntled with the runaway techno-marketing of the golf industry. It seems like a lot of the developments in golf clubs are more for the marketing impact than the playing impact. Modern clubs aren't really conducive to shaping shots. Golf is a game of finesse and I don't think it needs revolutionizing like a lot of people would have us believe. It has stood pretty well for a lot of years.

The business of golf deserves some attention.

It Costs How Much?

The tools of capitalism are everywhere. Courses feature full-color advertisements nestled in the bottom of the cup, on the dashboard of the golf cart, and on every tee sign. A golf course without a housing development is a rarity, or someone's mistake. Soon courses will boast carts equipped with instructional videos electronically programmed to provide just the swing tip you need, exactly when you need it. Already ProLink, SkyCaddie, PinMark, and Yardmark systems show green contours, exact yardage, hints from the course designer, and the wine list for the 19th hole on the cart's computer screen, all for your viewing pleasure while you lounge with your feet up on the dashboard and munch on a hot sandwich, your cell phone at your side.

To succeed in the free-market economy, courses have to be better than their competition. No longer is a course simply laid out on vacant land near town for locals. No sir, not anymore. Feasibility studies are done, environmental impact is measured, and earthmoving equipment is trucked in. This means extra expense for the owners, of course, with all the attendant costs passed on to the golfing consumer in one way or another. Many build a course to enhance housing projects. Instead of a walk in the park surrounded by trees, lakes, and the songs of birds, on these courses you traipse through other people's backyard barbecues. Golf carts often are necessary to get from the green to the next tee, located in another subdivision. At times you must drive on a suburban street, hustling down one driveway and up another to get from one hole to the next.

Owners market their courses to a target audience. As commodities, courses can be either high road, high volume, or high jinks. For example, Pebble Beach charges over $300 for one round of golf. It has greens and tees, bunkers and fairways like any other course. It also has the rocky Pacific shoreline, superb conditioning, unsurpassable vistas, enjoyable golf, and the image in every golfer's mind of Tom Watson chipping in on the 17th for his U.S. Open title. Even nongolfers can envision actor Jack Lemmon laboring through the last four holes on a Saturday, needing to birdie every one to make the pro-am cut. Pebble Beach is worth every penny, at least once in a lifetime. On the other hand, there are courses like PGA West that charge fees in the same high-price neighborhood as Pebble, but are really more like Uncle Ernie and his leisure suit—a lot of flash and not much else. What you get at PGA West is a typical desert course, an island green, a high slope rating, a lighter wallet, and a bunch of stories about how hard it was.

At the other end of the spectrum is the $5 course. Island Greens is on the south end of Whidbey Island, north of Seattle in Puget Sound. Locals call it Dave's Place. The hand-painted sign, nailed high in the tall pines, is easy to miss. So is the one-lane gravel drive. After parking in the dirt lot, you head toward the big pine tree. There, resting on a wooden shelf, is an iron pot with a slit in the top. Green fees are put in an envelope and stuffed through the slit. Three or four rough sets of rental clubs, $2.50, lean against the left side of the tree. Pull carts, a buck, wait on the right. All the money goes into the iron pot on the honor system. A gumball machine dispenses balls for 50 cents. It's nine holes, eight of them par-3s. The par-4 eighth is really a long par-3, but the severe green makes four a good score. Golf at Dave's Place is rough, simple, and as natural as can be. This course, too, is worth every penny.

Dave spends the time when he isn't fishing repairing ball marks on the greens. Most of his customers aren't aware of the damage their balls do to the putting surface and don't notice the holes and bumps as they putt. They are as blind to options as the players 150 years ago who drove off within two club lengths of the hole they just finished.

Some who play municipal courses don't know any better either. Their attitude is, "I paid my 30 bucks, so where's the first tee and how soon does the beer cart get here?" These fellows yell and hoot with every shot, good or bad. They take practice shots out of the sand, take divots with each of two to five practice swings, step on your line, and move and talk during your swing.

Such golfers are the target of corporate America. Marketing experts want them to buy more and play more. The challenge is to help these enthusiasts become more complete golfers and more enjoyable playing companions, to teach them that golf is worth the effort it takes to be knowledgeable about the game, and to make the game better, not worse—at a reasonable cost, of course.

Equipment

People gladly fork over hundreds of dollars for a Callaway driver. Some golf carts have onboard computers. Taylor Made's bubble shaft has a protrusion up near the grip. One wedge maker guarantees its special club will get you out of bunkers in one shot, every time. Some drivers will add 20 yards, others promise 40. Here are a few other recent touts for merchandise:

It's not made like other . . .
Most forgiving, letting you hit longer, straighter shots.
Bigger is better.
Quickly and almost automatically squares the face of
    the club at impact.
You'll hit the sweet spot no matter how you swing.

Sure it's hype, but we're buying it by the millions. A good product and better marketing increased the use of metal drivers from near-zero in the amateur ranks in 1986 to about 80 percent 10 years later. Ping, with Karsten Solheim as the Pied Piper of perimeter weighting, transformed the iron industry in half that time. Half the pros on tour use three wedges. What's hype? What's fad? What's real? Let's take an informed look at the technology waiting for you in the pro shop.

Art Chou, Peter Gilbert, and Tom Olsavsky (a trio of white-coated guys) conducted a series of tests to determine the facts about clubs. I'll start at the bottom, with clubheads. Is bigger really better? Yes, these scientists concluded. In irons, increased face size increases accuracy, increases launch angle, and increases spin. Furthermore, off-center hits are less off line. With drivers, the same is true: The larger the clubhead, the higher the ball flight and the more accurate the off-center hits. The only real downside, they report, is a tendency for the face to be open at impact, resulting in shots going to the right.

Perhaps the single most important club improvement in the last quarter century is perimeter weighting (although professional Willie Ogg thought to add lead weights to the toe of his irons back in 1933). Since it's a given that cavity-backed irons are more forgiving on off-center hits than the old blade, Chou et al. investigated this concept by moving weight around the perimeter of the clubhead to change the center of gravity, the critical element in trajectory and overall playability. Yes again, the trio chorus: improvement. A lower center of gravity shoots the ball higher with more spin: a higher center of gravity produces a lower flight with less spin. Go to your golf shop and buy what you need.

Offset—setting the clubface slightly in back of the shaft—has long been assumed to be a game-improvement feature. Chou, Gilbert, and Olsavsky looked at this, too. Yes again, they say. More offset, more loft, more backspin, and more hook spin.

Then there is gear effect: the action that occurs with off-center wood hits (even metal woods), mainly the driver. This effect exists because the center of gravity of woods is some distance away from the hitting surface. This doesn't occur in irons whose center of gravity is close to the clubface. What happens is that the off-center hit twists the wood clubhead around its center of gravity; a hit on the toe twists it open, a hit nearer the heel twists it closed. Think of gears: The twisting of the clubface causes the ball to spin in the opposite direction. For example, a heel hit rotates the clubface counterclockwise, and thus the ball clockwise, or with slice spin.

To compensate for this effect, wood-type clubs must be designed with a bulge so that the ball is forced to fly off line, with the gear-effect spin bringing it back toward the target. How much bulge to design in is determined by the club's center of gravity. Modern woods, made of metal, reduce the twisting of off-center hits due to increased perimeter weighting and a movable center of gravity (usually lower and more forward). You get higher shots and better misses with metal.

As far as the best distance among woods, metals, and composites is concerned, Clay Long, another one of those with calculator close at hand, reports "no difference." He goes on to say, "It is not the new material itself that is directly responsible [for better performance]. It's what the new material allows the manufacturer to do with the overall club design." Like bigger heads and longer shafts. And that's why all the hype. You really *can* buy an improved game in the pro shop.

But how much? Golf continues to be like Fi Fi LaBelle—teasing, showing, then taking away. One experiment between blade and cavity-backed irons found a 40 percent difference in accuracy using a 5-iron. The nod, of course, goes to the cavity-backed club when hit with mechanical hitting machine Iron Byron. With real golfers, the folks with pocket protectors equivocate. This is what Carl Scheie of Wilson Sporting Goods concludes:

> Although equipment can play a role in "improving" a player's game, the cause and effect relationships are neither straightforward nor universal. For example, changing to a more flexible shaft may cause one player to fade the ball more but another to draw it more. Either or both situations may result in improving performance—or the opposite.

Obviously, there is more to this equipment business than meets the eye. Let's continue upward from the clubhead to the connection of the head to the shaft where lie angle is created. Everyone agrees clubs that are too flat will cause the ball to be hit right; conversely, clubs that are too upright result in shots to the left. In addition, the higher the loft of the club, the greater the effect that lie angle will have on the direction of the ball. This is true no matter how expensive the clubs. Lie angle is one of the best-understood and most easily exhibited and fitted design features, unlike golf shafts.

Tom Wishon of Golfsmith International gives us fair warning. "When a golfer chooses a shaft," he says, "there has been no real way of knowing just what performance characteristics are contained within the shaft."

There are four shaft performance characteristics: weight, flex, torque, and bend point. The first is easy. The lighter the shaft, the greater the club speed; the result is increased distance. Sort of. A substantial reduction in shaft weight produces only a slight increase in clubhead speed, and consequently only a slight increase in distance.

Shaft flex is more interesting. Flex ratings, such as R for regular flex, do not necessarily equate to the R ratings given by other manufacturers and, often enough, they don't equate to R shafts of other types by the same manufacturer. What is known and pretty well universally accepted is that most players play too stiff a shaft, and would gain distance and satisfaction with a more flexible one. You're playing with too stiff a shaft if the ball doesn't travel as far when compared to other kinds of shafts, the ball flies too low, or there's a loss of feel or solidness of impact.

Torque, or propensity to twist, defines the shaft's resistance to twisting. The role torque has in the swing is getting the club square at impact. For the most part steel shafts have uniform torque; you can ignore the issue with these clubs. Graphite and other fiber shafts have varying torque and warrant close attention. However, the view can be narrow. The harder the swing, the lower the torque must be, supporting the converse idea that seniors and others with similar swings can benefit from the extra flip that torque can supply.

As for bend point, no one seems to know exactly how this should be measured, how results should translate into club fitting, and how much difference this factor makes in distance, accuracy, or anything else. Someone somewhere, though, is working on it.

An obvious element of shafts is length. Increasing length an inch or two does add distance, with some decrease in accuracy. Increasing more than a couple of inches doesn't seem to do much except produce more mis-hits and a few more stares from other golfers suddenly confronted by a fishing pole sticking out of your golf bag.

As for the grip, whatever feels good is fine. Some say grips that are too small will cause hits to the left and vice versa. Not always.

Finally, we are left with swing weight, an elusive concept of D4s, C8s, and such. Essentially, swing weight is a measurement of weight distribution around a fulcrum—or, perhaps more simply, of how heavy the clubhead feels. The letter-number combination is only a confusing way to define the total weight and relative heaviness of the clubhead. Your opinion of what is best is the correct one.

Of course, you could always make your own clubs.

Homemade Tools

One way to gain perspective on this equipment issue is to get in touch with the old ways by fashioning your own clubs. Few other games allow participants to make their own tools, and few activities teach more appreciation for what clubs can do than making them. One benefit of science has been the development of resins, polymers, epoxies, and the like; another the manufacturing advances that have allowed the marketing of club components. With these benefits, even the man who cannot change the sparkplugs in his car and the woman who isn't quite sure what a Phillips-head screwdriver is can successfully repair a club or build an entire set.

Start with an old 5-iron. Change the lie angle, alter the loft, add some lead tape, and see what happens. Grips can be changed as only one item on your Saturday-morning list of chores. Cut off the old one, put on an extra wrap for a different feel, slip on the new grip, let it dry for an hour, and let it rip. For less than $10 you can buy a book on club making by Golfsmith of Texas. GolfWorks runs a weeklong school.

Imagine the pleasure of finding an old persimmon driver in a barrel, dented, paint chipped, whipping unraveled: You take it home, repair its cracks, stain it, polish it up, put in a new shaft, balance it just perfectly, and use it next time you play. Would you enjoy it more than something store bought? Think you might hit it better?

It isn't much of a stretch to see how golf knowledge arises from the craftsmanship of club making, club repair, and club fitting. The player who uses his hands to create a new 7-iron, for example, knows that 7-iron, its hardness, the grooves, the loft, and the size of the face. And if he makes a 5-iron, too, he becomes well aware of the difference between the two clubs; he can feel it in his hands with a blindfold over his eyes. This awareness in turn becomes a true sense of what each club can do. Percy Boomer emphasized the ability to hit 70-yard shots with every club. The club maker can do this, for the club has become an extension of his hands.

Inside and Outside
the Golf Ball

Old Tom Morris left the employ of Allen Robertson because of the arrival of a new, improved golf ball. Robertson was not happy with Tom's interest in abandoning the old featherie for the attractive interloper, the gutta-percha, a natural hard-rubber-type material that could be molded into shape. It didn't take long, however, for the world's first golf professional to accept that the guttie was far superior, and around 1852 he also succumbed to making them. It was cheaper, more durable, more consistent, and longer than its predecessor once it was roughed up during play. Since then, golf-ball development has shortened courses and ballooned the distance amateurs claim for their everyday tee shots.

The advance on the guttie was the Haskell, a rubber-core ball developed by Coburn Haskell and Bertram Work. This ball really could add 30 yards to the drive of an average player. John Low, a traditionalist, complained of the unfair advantage weaker players enjoyed, especially when they too would be able to reach long par-4s in two. Defenders of the ball suggested simply building longer holes for this new age. By 1915 the rubber-core ball was decreed by all to be more enjoyable to play, and the days of the guttie were over.

According to Alastair Cochran, the Royal and Ancient's former technical director, the uniformity of the modern ball is one of the great advances of the game. So is, he would agree, the scientific approach to designing covers and cores to fit almost every need. From the thickness, and hardness of cover materials to core materials, dimple patterns, ball sizes, and even the ratio of dimples to smooth surface, the choice of which golf ball to play has leapt from using whatever is in the bag to a computerized match-making of ball, player, course, and conditions. Course is long, day windy, greens of average softness and size? Then choose a moderately hard cover with a soft core. You'll get less spin and more run, yet retain stopping power for approaches to the green. Playing a tight course with small greens and your handicap is 12 to 21? Pick a two-piece medium polyurethane-ionomer cover. Enough distance, but with spin to hold the green.

And there's more.

The critical factors in golf balls are the hardness and thickness of the cover and the core. A larger ball so far hasn't proven to be of much benefit. (It's legal to play any ball that's 1.68 inches or more in diameter—girth being limited, one assumes, only by the diameter of the hole.) Compression, such as 100, 90, or 80, which are standard but relatively inaccurate measures, means very little in ball performance.

Cover hardness directly affects spin rate. The softer the cover, the more spin. Conversely, the softer the core, the less spin. If you'd like a ball that spins less to better control your slice, for example, your choice is a hard cover over a soft core. More spin to maneuver the ball or to gain stopping power requires a hard core and soft cover.

Distance is affected by the thickness of the cover. The cover (and the core) must be highly resilient to the blow made by the club. The more the club's energy can be retained, the greater the distance. Soft cover materials tend to absorb energy. A thin cover over a hard core is one way of minimizing energy loss; so is a thick, hard cover.

Another misunderstood event is how the ball acquires spin. Sliding up the clubface is not the cause; nor are the grooves on the club, square or otherwise. What causes spin is how the ball temporally sticks to the clubface, due to the combined effect of cover and core, and how it rebounds off the angled clubface. Any pro could tell you that.

The Professionals

There are golf people you should talk to. Find a few local club pros and chat with them a while, even invite them to lunch. These folks know a ton about the inner workings of golf. Most can tell you about clubs and balls, swing mechanics, the markup on soft goods, running tournaments, cart maintenance, and a little something about course management. Few, however, know who Willie Park was; fewer still Bill Spiller or even Joseph C. Dey. The working professional is busy. The pressures of running a business, and the rewards of doing so, seem to first erode the pure joys of golf, then supplant them. Still, these are the men and women who run most of the golf courses. They need our support and encouragement. Talk to them. Buy from them. Take a lesson.

Full-time teaching professionals, especially the ones at weeklong schools, have the luxury of a broader view, and many are willing and able to sit and chat with students after formal instruction. Most who become golf professionals, as opposed to professional golfers, do so because they love the game. (A surprising number of professional players, by the way, cite competition as the main reason they play—and they don't play for fun during their free time.) Teachers enjoy introducing others to golf and furthering competence.

Other groups of workers well worth your time are course superintendents and the members of grounds crews. These folks can tell you stories of what happens on the course that will amaze and disappoint. You will hear what damage angry players do to the cup after a miss. The odd items found in the trash cans. Deep, ball-sized dents in the wooden tee signs. Beer cans left in the crotches of trees, condoms in the bunkers, and cigar butts on the tees. More reasons to protect the game.

Make time to have lunch with the super. Learn about drainage, fungi that attack the greens, and how tough it can be to schedule routine maintenance. The course you play takes hundreds of hours of upkeep to look good.

Things were different in the old days. Horace Hutchinson, prior to World War I, described the height of decadence at Westward Ho! during the era when rain watered the grass and sheep mowed it. "I am not quite sure that we did not think we had done a very big thing, almost gone too far on the lines of luxury and precise attention to having all in perfect order," he said, "when one of the members sent to Scotland for a hole cutter." Until then the hole was simply a hole everyone putted to until its edges became too mangled or the hole too deep. Then a new one was dug nearby.

Look at the course from the inside out. See the underpinnings of the game and understand what a complex operation a golf course is, especially with modern-day regulations and player expectations. How do you want it—manicured as neat and pretty as 10 pink fingernails, or more like the place Mr. Hutchinson might have played?

4

THROUGH THE GREEN

The Best Course in the World

Pine Valley, the George Crump design south of Phila-
delphia, is the best golf course in the world. The clubhouse is reminiscent of a hunting lodge that's a little frayed
at the edges. According to some visitors, the locker room
might have been the work of someone more used to designing bus stations. The bunkers aren't raked. The grounds are
unkempt.

The greens are nice, though, and the routing is through
some of the best golf land in the world. Pine Valley lays it all
out in front of you, "Here I am," it says, "try and beat me."
Pretend you can hit the ball 1 percent better than you can
and the course will turn you into turtle soup. Knowing its
reputation, a bunch of Arnold Palmer's friends once offered
him a wager. He would pay out $100 for every stroke over
80, and collect the same amount for every stroke under 72.
He was young, was not well off, had never played the course
before, and was in love. He won enough to buy his sweet-
heart Winnie a beautiful diamond engagement ring. The
rest, as they say, is history.

The course is as beautiful as it is deadly. But is it better
than Pebble Beach, the Old Course at St. Andrews, Cypress
Point, and every other course in the world? Jack Nicklaus
wouldn't choose to play his last round here. A lot of people
wouldn't.

In reality, there is no "best" course, shot values and every
other kind of golf value being as personal as they are. There
are courses that have the best overall shot values for the
widest range of players. There are courses that are the best

for good players, and there are best courses for bad players. There are courses for those looking for thrills. There are courses of almost impossible beauty. Ones ripe for scoring. Others so steeped in history you hesitate to take a divot.

Golf Digest in its list of the 100 best courses has an armful of criteria. But don't be swayed by the weight of experts and lists of well-defined parameters. Identifying the best course is like holding up an oil lamp and looking for the best spouse, or the best wine, or the best golf ball. Best is not inherent in the course but inside of you, part of the link between expectation and experience. Best is not made up from the collective elements of the course. It arises from your ability to appreciate their quality and balance, to feel them during play, and to remain awed for a long time after. That can happen anywhere. Judge a course from your experience—it's the only one that counts.

The Course

From Pine Valley or Dave's informal place on Whidbey Island to the silk carpet of Augusta National, stormy Machrihanish on the wild west coast of Scotland, and the quiet splendor of the Cascades in the misty mountains of Virginia, a golf course can be just about anything. Let's poke under the surface to gain true knowledge of what the course we love to play is all about.

The golf course has no inherent shape. It has evolved to consist of 18 tees and 18 holes, but in between anything and everything goes. In its purest form the golf course was created hole by hole as players wandered over links land and either found or dug holes at interesting intervals, and however many happened to fit. The original links courses were formed near estuaries, where fescue and bentgrass grew over rolling dunes of windblown sand. Stiff grass blades that could support a ball and the varied terrain combined to make the perfect conditions for a golfer to dig a hole and start playing. Often stone walls, streams, rocks, bushes, railway lines, and a host of other "natural" hazards added spice to play. As this land has become scarce, we have had to design new golf courses and build them to specification. For a while these manufactured courses mimicked the old, and if they were built on something other than sandy soil, like clay, they were often disasters. But the migration of courses from Scotland to England and on to the rest of the world could not be stopped by mere unsuitability of land. Heather and other intrusive bushes were soon removed, as were fir and pine trees. The trees and shrubs that were left created visual interest and strategic routing. Some earth had to be moved to build tees and greens, and grass had be sown. Purists of the day scoffed at any course not built on links land, but were soon convinced by the playability of inland heathland courses. Sunningdale and Walton Heath in England and Gleneagles in Scotland are prime examples of enjoyable links-land transplants.

Perhaps because builders were afraid of producing boring courses, early designs were of the penal variety, with fairway cross bunkers and greens surrounded by pot bunkers. Hired for a few pounds, a famous professional golfer would traipse around the grounds early in the day followed by boys carrying stakes. A gruff word and one stake would mark the tee; 100 paces were marched off and another was pounded in to mark the cross bunker. Farther on he would point to where another bunker would go, or perhaps two or three mounds, and a boy would put in more stakes. A few more steps and the green would be marked. A course designed in less than a day. Course features, one imagines, were limited only by the number of stakes or boys to carry them. More was better.

Developed in the great days of penal golf, Oakmont was designed and constructed by Henry Fownes at the beginning of the 20th century. Later his son William decided to make it into the toughest layout in the world. "A shot poorly played should be a shot irrevocably lost" was his motto. Two hundred twenty bunkers, an average of 12 per hole, provided a good start. Then to add insult to misery, he and his greenkeeper "Dutch" Loeffler developed the famed heavy rake to press furrows into the thick, heavy sand. Greens were razored and rolled, then coated with thin sheets of glass.

Time and another look at the best natural courses taught even the Calvinists that strategic golf was more interesting. Oakmont, for example, later filled in some bunkers and relegated the rakes to a museum. Most courses today are of the strategic variety, with variety the operational concept.

Mother Nature, the first designer, had no competition and no concern about being outdone or winning another commission. The designers who followed have not enjoyed the same luxury. Human nature being what it is, if one created a course with gently rolling greens, the next had to increase the undulations, or make deeper bunkers, or even place one of the greens in the middle of a lake or shape it like a pineapple. The last 100 years have seen the creation of a number of bad courses, yet also signs of the maturity of design. The best designers are beginning to lose their love of trademark affectations in favor of working hand in hand with Mother Nature.

For a complete and fascinating look at the design and construction of a course, *Driving the Green* by John Strawn should be read cover to cover and from discovery of the building site to the first putt.

Inside the Course

At the risk of making the Old Course at St. Andrews too much of a shrine, it is worth another visit to establish a benchmark. "Magical," writer Dick Taylor and a thousand others have said of it, with "a mystique, an aura, no other place possesses." Yet it is only grass. There are rolling fairways and double greens, to be sure, but just 18 holes, three trees (small), one water hazard in play (Swilken Burn on the first hole), a few infamous bunkers, and a lot of history. When Sam Snead first saw it through the window of a train he thought it was an abandoned golf course. As links land it has a great variety of slopes, making for interesting ball positions: Rarely do you have a level lie. The sandy subsoil drains quickly. The topsoil supports a perfect grass for hitting a golf ball. All natural. Pits worn by animals and exposed sand dunes became bunkers. Holes are placed in relatively "flat" spots on an otherwise boiling landscape. And that's pretty much it.

Of course, it's what happens inside us that makes St. Andrews what it is. Course designer Robert Hunter described as well as anyone playing this old place:

> There is something in the very terrain which outwits us. . . . We never have sufficient variety of shots or quite enough skill and accuracy to play St. Andrews as we should like to play it, or indeed as we feel that one day we should play it. That is, I think, what gives the Old Course its enduring vitality. It is the most captivating and unfair, the most tantalizing and bewitching, of all courses.

But that was way back in the hickory-club era, the "old type of golf" of MacKenzie, "in which a player has no fixed line to the hole." What trouble an architect would be in today if he produced a course like the Old at St. Andrews.

And why is that?

Shot Values

A benchmark much in use nowadays is the concept of shot values. Basically, this means the relative difficulty of a shot and the concomitant interest or boredom of the player. The challenge for course architects is to produce optimum shot values for every level of player, to do so with varying techniques, and in a smoothly flowing sequence. The best ones do a good job, but we have lost something by allowing designers to provide chef's specials rather than Mother Nature's menu of choices. It is probably obvious to you by now that in days past, before many courses expressed the creative concepts of designers and owners, shot values were created on the fly by the golfer himself as he worked his way toward the green. In those days of yore imagination was one of the more important core values in golf. This not the case much now, especially in the United States, where imagination is no longer useful after first-tee handicap negotiations.

A good hole is one designed to be enjoyable for everyone, no matter how talented. This is a tall order. Expectations play a central role. Those who play a draw will judge courses with a lot of doglegs to the right to be poorly designed. Likewise, extensive carries discourage short hitters. However, as long as the hole does not demand the impossible for any player and the course does not favor any one type of shot, a wise player should be able to find enjoyment. An important component of shot values is the player's character, and character is greatly influenced by knowledge.

Professionals are notorious for criticizing courses that take the driver out of their hands or feature odd landing areas, as if the holes should respond to their games rather than the other way around. A good hole, and a good course, should be an examination that isn't easy to pass. If a hole appears unfair or to have poor shot values, make sure you have perceived the hole without bias. Few have the ability to fairly judge a hole they haven't yet played well.

The par-5 17th at Valderrama in Spain is reported to be a world-class example of a bad hole. Seve Ballesteros, who designed it, describes the hole as "beautiful, the trademark hole for the course." Critics, many of them European Tour players, complain that the landing area was ruined by a 10-yard-wide band of rough across the fairway, and that the green is both too narrow and too hard. It didn't help the reputation of the hole or its design when well-struck balls rolled back into the pond during an international tournament there in 1999, especially Tiger Woods's approach during the final round.* "Too fluky," they said. However, some made pars, some made birdies, and all played the same hole. These comments raise the issue of how to define "too" of anything on a golf course.

---

*Tiger's composure with his ball rolling, not spinning, into the water was truly remarkable.

Modern Courses

These are some of the changes that have occurred to "modernize" golf courses—despite the fact that the average golfer's handicap has stayed pretty much the same for the past 20 years:

- Championship courses have been stretched by about 500 yards.
- More and deeper bunkers are constructed because of how well professionals have learned to manage them.
- Greens have become larger due to increased traffic, and flatter due to the popularity of fast greens.
- Fairways are flatter because we expect them to be, they are easier to maintain, and they are more "fair."
- Hazards and even fairways have an artificial appearance, which makes them easier to construct and maintain; also, we've come to accept it.

There is a philosophy at work that's much different from the antiquated practice of discovering golf holes in an open field. There are no more open fields. We have laws, commercial interests, and, most important, expectations. According to course construction writer John Strawn:

> Americans wanted the ambiguity out of golf . . . perfectly maintained fairways from tee to green, mechanically groomed sand bunkers, and greens smooth as the surface of a pool table, with the route of play firmly within planned corridors.

Public land is scarce and must be used for multiple purposes. Private land is expensive and also must be multitasked. Courses are built to make money. To do that, they must meet players' expectations. This requires a lot of thought and a lot of hard work.

There are a few design principles that everyone tries to follow, such as minimizing holes that line up toward the rising or setting sun, placing 1st and 10th holes near the pro shop, starting off with easier holes to get things moving, and avoiding impossible carries.*

Then come the more subtle or not-so-subtle features. One concern is how much an architect's style should be recognizable. A great novel is often defined as one in which the reader is unaware of the writer and becomes totally absorbed in the characters and plot; the beauty of the words and the construction of the story are noticed only upon rereading or with concentrated study. Should a golf course be the same? Can the player become so engrossed in figuring out the challenges, be so connected to the course that only later, or with repeated play, do design features become apparent? That would worry owners who pay high fees for a Nicklaus signature course, or a Dye or Jones layout. (They can expect a premium of 120 percent over a course designed by a lesser name.) There must be instant recognition of these great names, otherwise big bucks have been wasted. Fewer will pay high green fees, stay in the hotel, or buy the expensive building lots.

Drainage is basic and critically important, because it affects everything, from the type of grass that can be grown

---

*The wisdom of minimizing carries was demonstrated with *Golf Digest*'s "Worst Avid Golfer" contest in 1985. Four men were selected to play the Tournament Players Course from the tips. Eventual winner Angelo Spangnolo "won" with a 257 when he couldn't meet the challenge of the par-3 17th—the island green. After the group put dozens of balls into the water, he ended up bunting his ball around the pond and down the walkway to the putting surface.

to elevation changes and the positioning of holes, hazards, and even clubhouse. A green isn't simply a green but a water-storage receptacle that must be drained in such a way as to look natural and attractive, flow toward established drainage basins, and dry quickly. A pond is not only a body of water but also a scenic view from the clubhouse, a forced carry, a strategic decision, a drainage basin, a water supply, and a habitat for fish, fowl, flora, and as many of the fauna as can be designed in.

When a golf course is being planned, the end result of a playable course involves creating functional harmony among natural features, the prevailing weather, and as many of man's resources as necessary. David Boocock of Britain's Sports Turf Research Institute summarized the situation this way:

> Total nutritional and irrigation requirements have to be provided and maintained in an artificial situation which always puts turf grasses under stress from frequent mowing and the constant wear, abrasion and compaction which results from play. Maintenance of such a turf is constantly balanced on a knife-edge.

Golf courses take up 2,500 square miles of land in the United States, 10 million acres worldwide. Courses use valuable space, water, human resources, and deadly chemicals. The land must be bulldozed, dirt contoured, miles of irrigation trenches dug, tons of pea gravel and top-dressing smoothed out, and grass sown and grown. And there's more.

While the residents of Scotland had only to dig a hole to play golf, modern developers have to contend with financing, permits, access roads, allowable densities, yellow horned toad mating sites, squeezed-in housing lots, paved cart paths, a few golf holes, and creating just the right ambience to sell memberships fast enough to turn a profit. It should be no surprise that golf is driven by factors other than the simple joy of an afternoon's recreation. Too much is at stake.

Mark Massara, an environmental attorney, took the golf industry to task in a 1996 *GOLFWEEK* article. "Contemporary golfing," he says, "requires hundreds of acres of artificial super-lawn, thousands of gallons of water per day, and thousands of pounds of chemicals annually." His opinion is strong. Golf, he says, is losing its taking-nature-as-it-comes orientation and has been "reduced to an experience rather like schlepping through a strip mall. The problem," he continues, "is that golf has been co-opted, kidnapped, hijacked and manipulated by real estate speculators, chemical manufacturers and golf course architects and designers." To Mr. Massara golf, that grand old game of playing the ball as you find it, has sold out. High green fees disqualify too many enthusiasts. In underdeveloped countries native populations are evicted from their land, even killed, while farming land is lost to build a golf resort. He has solutions: Abandon courses built on poor sites, eliminate chemicals, use less water, and don't build so much.

The superintendent's early-evening spreading of chemicals to keep his course in optimum green condition has become an international crisis. With, unfortunately, good reason. Jim Hansen, chairman of Auburn University's history department and a technology expert, is "not optimistic that golfers are going to change their perspective about playing conditions. I don't really find golfers all that interested in moving away from the kind of playing conditions that they now identify as being the best golf."

The complaint about golf is that courses take up valuable land, disrupt natural habitats, pollute water supplies, and use up other resources. No one can disagree that construction and maintenance of golf courses can cause these problems. Valuable wetlands were unthinkingly filled with dirt to make a longer par-5 and a better par-3 green at Boyne Highlands. Almost 200 Canada geese bodies once littered the fairways of the Sewane Club on Long Island, dead from pesticide poisoning. The Arizona desert has become a golfing greenbelt, draining the aquifer so that some nearby wells have dried up. In other places well water near golf courses has been tainted.

Dr. Mike Kenna, director of the USGA's Green Section, believes that golf should not be about attractiveness but "about playability; it should be about protecting and encouraging the natural environment." The USGA has formed two conservation projects, the Audubon Cooperative Sanctuary Program and the Wildlife Links program, to do just that. The first helps courses become mini ecosystems by emphasizing habitat management, conservation, and environmental planning. Course superintendents register for the program and take an inventory of resources. A conservation report is compiled to act as a guide, the project is implemented, and, with hard work, a course becomes certified. The result has been course areas left in their natural state where songbirds sing and wildflowers bloom. Although not as formal, the Wildlife Links program does the same thing by helping courses retain features that enable animals and golfers to cohabit. With both programs, players soon get used to deer and other wildlife becoming part of the golf experience.

Farther on the plus side are the actual benefits of a golf course for the environment. Few would say that an abandoned strip mine was more attractive than the golf course that replaced it. No one complains when a course is constructed in otherwise unusable land as part of a housing development. And this kind of improvement has happened in a number of places.

James Beard of the International Sports Turf Institute has a lot of reasons to praise the ecological benefits of golf, most of which hardly anyone thinks about. One is water retention. Golf-course turf reduces erosion and essentially traps water runoff so that it filters into the water table. Groundwater quality is improved by the biodegradation of natural and artificial organic compounds common to modern living. The normal activities of turf, like photosynthesis and decay, add to general soil improvement. Golf-course grasses help dissipate heat, absorb noise, and actually reduce glare. And as I have discussed, the less closely mowed areas can provide a home for all sorts of creatures.

Mother Nature has thrown down the gauntlet: We are either part of the problem or part of the solution. Soon golfers will have to learn to coexist with the demands and limitations of nature, invent new grasses and techniques to grow them, or continue the movement toward artificial devices, such as manufactured tees and greens. One good solution is to do them all. Players may one day be able to play a regulation course, sometimes brown in the summer, that fits into the ecosystem without a hitch. Other courses may be covered in hybrid grasses, painted green in the summer, that grow only with expensive pampering. Smaller executive courses played with a regular golf ball may compete with similar-length layouts designed to be played with the shorter-flying Cayman ball. Golf may become a set of games depending on the time and interests of the players.

Grass

A major golf problem is grass—growing it and maintaining it to golfing standards, especially on greens. According to architect Tom Doak, "The choice of grasses is as important to the golf course as the choice of upholstery to the interior designer." From among the hundreds of grasses, only a few can tolerate the foot traffic, divots, ball marks, cutting, and constant intrusion of weeds and disease all common on the golf course.

I shall not dig into the details of modern agronomy, but an elementary understanding of the complexities of turf will enable us to defend against unwarranted attacks and help shape the direction of course maintenance. Would we be willing, for example, to promote brown grass greens in exchange for less water use, lower fees, and more water-friendly neighborliness? Using greens as the focal point, there are many issues to discuss.

Some soils are better for some grasses, and some climates also favor one type of grass over another. What is native to a region is usually a good bet. But some courses have many types of soils, and with giant earthmovers, almost anything can be hauled in and given a try. Making a mistake in what is attempted can be a disaster, as attested to by the chronic problems at Riviera in Los Angeles, where green construction, type of grass, maintenance, and weather combined to produce greens that are almost unplayable. Wise golfers will understand and accept the limitations inherent in the land, and will not expect Augusta-type greens in Tucson, Milwaukee, or anywhere else for that matter.

Golfers will have to realize that Augusta greens are not the appropriate benchmark for appearance. American TV viewers are surprised to see brown greens during many British Opens and amused to see the dust fly with every iron shot. This is a major championship, they think; it shouldn't be this way. But these courses are of top quality and usually in terrific shape. Greens that are a deep rich color and closely cut are like the stereotypical bad girl wearing heavy makeup and a short, tight skirt: headed for trouble.

Good greens are not easy to achieve. Cutting the grass regularly encourages healthy growth and reduces leaf size and coarseness. Frequent mowing smooths the surface and provides the consistency golfers want. The height of the cut must be a compromise, however. Low cuts provide tournament-type greens but lessen the antidamage cushion of deeper grass, weaken root strength and growth, and may allow native species of weeds and grasses to take hold.

The favored sibling to consistency is speed, the crowning glory of many private clubs and upscale resort courses that promote U.S. Open–type greens. Speed is a combination of grass type, very low mowing (the 1999 U.S. Open at Pinehurst 2 aimed at 0.135 inch), fertilization, and green hardness. With some variation due to subsoil types, less watering, less fertilizer, and less grass lead to the fastest putting speeds. In other words, greens near death are the kind many course superintendents are expected to maintain month after month.

But those white-coated folks are on top of this issue. Penn A-4, developed at Penn State, promises to stand up to tournament length of ⅛ inch or less. Pete Dye says, "It will change the whole complexion of golf." It's tough, he reports, and "still slicker than wet linoleum." I wonder if proliferation of this grass might eventually become golf's version of the gift of nuclear energy.

Golfers also want greens to be soft, balls flying in and sticking quick. This can be done with more feeding, more water, and longer grass. No one knows for sure just what hardness golfers favor most, but the ideal should be what's best for the green.

Greens have to be durable—able to withstand size-13 shoes, 200-pound players, metal spikes, skidding golf balls, late-night frosts, heavy mowers, constant cutting, and a few angry golfers. The trend toward soft spikes is a good one. Walking carefully is also helpful, as is patience during frost delays and fixing your ball mark—and two or three others as well.

The putting surface must be able to recover from damage quickly, before individual roots die from too little or too much water, inappropriate fertilization, or even constant mowing. And it must be relatively easy to maintain. Thatch, a natural accumulation of surface debris and a natural cushion for ball and feet, increases with fertilizers and watering. Footprints and slow greens are the result. Verticutting—using a machine with thin vertical blades—cuts and removes much of the thatch at the same time.

Obviously, keeping greens in good condition requires balancing many factors and considerable planning and work. There are two rules of thumb. The fewer chemical additions and the more nature can nurture, the better. And the more golfers learn about greens and grasses, and accept the limitations of Mother Nature, the better it will be for the greens and the game.

For more information about greens and greenkeeping, contact the USGA or the National Golf Foundation (see Resources on page 209). Both have excellent publications you may buy. Or check out Tom Doak's *The Anatomy of a Golf Course* for a bigger picture.

5

THE GOLF STROKE

Brains, Grace, and Rhythm

To swing respectably well requires little intelligence and even less knowledge. Children of five can mimic Tiger Woods, yet not fathom placeholders or have a clue how to spell *Minneapolis*. To score well takes a little more brain power, but not much. In fact, the more intelligent the player, the more some of that excess intelligence has to be used to overcome the confounding effects of thinking. Walter Hagen once said, "Give me a man with big hands, big feet and no brains and I will make a golfer out of him." Everything must be in harmony to play well, including brawn and brain. Too much physical effort produces tension and a bad golf stroke. Too much brain power induces paralysis, panic, confusion, or a hurried swing just to release 1,000 gigahertz of tension.

In golf, for the most part, less is more. Picture the simple beauty of Michelangelo's *David*, the slow grace of the Japanese tea ceremony, or the captivating smoothness of a waltz. Balance. Rhythm. Harmony. Union of mind and body. These should be the foundation of your swing. Once everything works together, the swing is sure to be a good one.

One way to do this is to imagine that your swing is like an old-fashioned record player, able to be played at either 33⅓, 45, or 78 rpm. Your natural tempo can be slow, medium, or fast; it doesn't matter. Timing and rhythm do. As long as your entire swing is played at the correct speed, it will make sweet music. But try to swing harder or with extra emphasis on one part or another and your swing will more resemble the sound of fingernails on a blackboard.

It is never how hard. It is always how well.

Hips, Shoulders, and Wrists

The golf swing is comprised of two levers. One is your arms, with the fulcrum somewhere between your spine and your sternum. The second lever is the club, with the fulcrum at your wrists. The idea is to manage these two levers so they combine efficiently. Most poor golfers seem to believe that a powerful golf stroke comes from swinging the arms as fast as possible. Unless they are timed with the second lever of the wrists and club, however, fast arms are more for show than effect.

The lever of the arms, like a pendulum, must be brought back as far as possible. Do this by turning the shoulders so the middle of your back is facing the target. The club lever is powered by a wrist cock during the backswing, and a release (your right hand, or more accurately right forearm, turning over your left) on the downswing. The combination of these two levers, timed correctly, is what produces a good swing. A third lever, the elbows (consciously bending and unbending), could apply a modicum of increased power but in reality usually causes things to go haywire. Comfortably firm but not stiff arms produce maximum power and consistency.

The hips transfer momentum from one side of the body to the other. The force of the swing comes from efficiently transferring this momentum to the arms, then to the clubhead, and hence to the ball. The fewer the extra moves or compensations during this transference, the better your swing. For example, many players lift the club rather than turn the body on the backswing. This is done because it's easier. Lifting on the backswing usually adds the compensation of dropping the left (or forward) shoulder. To compensate for the first compensation, the downswing must include a lifting motion or a shift to the right—what's called a reverse weight shift. The result is neither pretty nor effective.

The wrists, important as the fulcrum for the second (club) lever, also are compensation trouble spots. Without a good grip, which can freely release, every other part of the swing must become part of a series of adjustments and compromise. And to repeat: Every compensation reduces swing efficiency.

Release is a great term. Think you should be relaxed for a good release?

One Move, Only One

At the least a swing is comprised of grip, stance, swing plane, arc, wrist cock, arms, shoulders, head position, feet, legs, balance, timing, rhythm, speed, weight shift, release, and follow-through. It is also the generation of about 4 horsepower by one little human being within little more than a second, to swing a clubhead at 100 miles an hour, to hit a spot the size of a nickel more than a yard from the swing center, to reach a target often 200 yards away. Bio-psycho-mechanically, reaching Mars in a manned spacecraft might be easier.

The best names in teaching say the same thing. Harvey Penick of the Red and the Green books reminds us that "the turn is a natural movement of the body, and your bones are connected from the ground up." He means that the swing has many parts, but that they're connected and are a series of automatically combined pieces. This concept is echoed by former British Women's Open Champion Vivian Saunders: "The golf swing is essentially a whole movement and must always be seen as such." She rightly admonishes us for our almost obsessive interest in all the pieces of the swing and gently but clearly warns, "Any teaching method which over-fragments the swing is in many ways psychologically very clever and yet from a performance point of view totally disastrous."

No one has demonstrated the overfragmentation of the golf swing better than John Updike in his article "Drinking from a Cup Made Cinchy," subtitled "After Reading Too Many Books on How to Play Golf." He instructs the reader in the fine art of drinking a cup of tea exactly the way a golf pro might teach how to hit a simple chip shot. Here is a portion of part two of step one, receiving the cup from the hostess:

> In seizure, first touch, with feathery lightness, the rim of the saucer with the pad of the index finger of the right hand. A split second—perhaps .07—later, the first knuckle of the middle, "big" finger, sliding toward the center of the saucer's invisible under-side, and the tip of the thumb must coordinate in a prehensile "pinching" motion. This motion must occur. The two remaining fingers of the right hand of necessity accompany the big finger, but should not immediately exert pressure, despite their deep seated instinct to do so. Rather, the wrist is gently supinated. . . .

And from Bob Jones, "The first requisite of a truly sound swing is simplicity."

In the misty days of the featherie and whippy wooden shafts, the golf swing was a wonder of swaying body, flying elbows, and a sweeping stroke, all the better to control the club and loft the featherie into the air with minimum damage to ball, club, and player. As clubs became stiffer and, in the 1930s, were made of steel, the swing evolved into more of a hit. With the advent of modern materials, the accepted standard is to hold the club primarily in your fingers, take it back to parallel or a little less, then use the large muscles of your legs and trunk to initiate the downswing while allowing centrifugal force to release your hands.

To fully understand the golf swing, it is useful to know exactly what it is supposed to accomplish. A good swing has three characteristics: It produces speed, is accurate, and is repeatable. These three characteristics are essentially equal. Focus too much on speed and one or both of the other factors are affected. The same holds true for an overemphasis on accuracy or consistency. If you can manage these characteristics to some degree, though, you'll be able to achieve the three magic goals: hit the ball far enough to do some good, close enough to the target to score well, and often enough to enjoy the game. A good blend of all three, of course, produces wonderful results.

The only place where speed is important is in the club-head. Not the hands. Not the arms. Not the legs. The idea is to have the clubhead accelerating as it reaches the ball, theoretically reaching its top speed at a point just after impact. Strangely enough, this is done by the arms slowing down, which allows your hands to release, thus speeding the clubhead through the hitting area. The force of the hit is determined by the mass of the clubhead and its acceleration (as opposed to velocity). Or as you may remember from physics class way back when, $F = m \times a$, with a equal to velocity squared! Those vicious swings by the gorillas of the game look strong but they're pansies compared to a smooth swing of the arms timed with a good release. Effortless power.

If your wrists release too soon, as is often the case with poorer golfers, the dual effect is completely lost and the clubhead is virtually pushed at the ball with little or no acceleration. This tendency is part of what's called casting. It's often the cause of out-to-in swing paths and the all-too-common slice. This is where patience and "waiting for the swing" are helpful.

Consistency is the result of sensations. Sensing the swing and being comfortable with how it feels increase the likelihood that your next swing will be similar to the last. Sensations can be affected by trying to increase swing speed, the tension of a match, trying a new grip, and a lot of other distractions. Anything that affects the sensation of the swing will alter it, almost always in a negative way. Percy Boomer, a top player and teacher in the 1920s, had this to say:

> You have to learn [golf] and play it through your senses. You must be mindful but not thoughtful as you swing. You must not think or reflect; you must feel what you have to do. Part of the diffi-

culty arises because, apart from simple things like riding a bicycle, we have never learned to do things in this way.

What Boomer thought were the most important elements to sense are the pivot (with the hips), the shoulders rotating in response to the pivot, and the arms moving in response to the shoulders—all as one unit and as a unified feel of the swing.

Harvey Penick describes Scottish golfer MacDonald Smith's swing this way:

> His swing was full and flowing and graceful. I wouldn't know how else to describe it. It didn't break down into parts any more than a wonderful poem breaks down into words.

Swing like that.

Facts and Fallacies

"You don't hit the ball with the backswing" sounds logical and true. But don't believe it. If you sense the swing as a unit, it starts with taking the club away from the ball. Many teachers advocate taking the clubhead back "low and slow" to encourage a full extension on the backswing. Research suggests that doing so with a shoulder turn, then adding a lift of the arms, produces the optimum swing path. Few amateurs pay attention to the backswing; few professionals don't.

"A full coil produces the most power" has been around a long time and is a destructive concept. "Coiling" promotes a buildup of tension. Golfers are not rubber bands. Muscles don't stretch and rebound; they contract and pull. To reach the top of the backswing, some of your muscles must tighten and others must relax. Same thing with the downswing. Fred Couples is a wonderful example of a relaxed swing. He appears only to lift the club and let it fall.

The arms can start the downswing, so can the hands, and so can the legs. Different golfers at the highest levels have begun the downswing in all sorts of ways. However, one classic concept—"the swing starts from the ground up"—is true. In a closely timed series, the most efficient downswings are initiated with the right foot, followed by a strong push with the legs, turning hips, the back and chest accelerating the arms, the right shoulder dipping underneath the swing, and the wrists unhinging just prior to impact. The backswing does not build up power but sets up the correct swing plane so that all the complicated elements of the swing can unfold the right way. The backswing should be very relaxed. Two highly respected researchers of the swing, John Stobbs and Alastair Cochran, described the swing this way in 1968: "The legs and hips are the engine of the swing; the arms and hands are the transmission." And remember, engines don't have to be large if they're connected to the right set of gears.

Ken Venturi, a former U.S. Open champion and later a golf commentator, once remarked on how he played the 10th hole at the Riviera Country Club, a par-4 of just over 300 yards. He said that when he tried to drive the green, striking the shot as hard as he possibly could, his results were usually bad. The one time he used a driver with the intention of laying up, his relaxed swing put the ball on the green. He learned an important lesson about swinging within himself. A quietly purring motor will maximize the probability of everything working well on the downswing. It doesn't work to play a 33⅓ record at 78.

"Hit hard with the right side" is another common idea. The fact is, a firm grip with your left hand and gentle guidance with your right throughout the swing produce the best results. A freewheeling lever is the idea, and a freewheeling (relaxed) hinge at your wrists helps you do that.

One old saw that's fast losing favor is "keep your head still." The idea behind keeping the head still is to keep the swing plane constant so that the low point on your downswing will be the same at impact as it was at address; in addition, the weight shift can focus power. It's a good concept, but keeping your head still is the wrong way to achieve the desired results. The heads of many good players actually move backward as the club arrives at impact. The central chest area should remain stable, although it certainly turns during the swing. Moving your upper body forward during the downswing would lessen the lever effect, and the swing would become more of a push.

It is not known who first described this way to swing, but it may be this is the image to keep in mind: "Swing as if the ball were a dandelion."

Improving Your Score

Many players believe the secret to better scoring is in putting. Not so. Lou Riccio of Golf Analyzer tells us what to look for. Dr. Riccio analyzed over 60,000 strokes from golfers of all levels to determine what kinds of shots most affect scores.

Most highly correlated to scoring was the familiar "greens in regulation." No matter what his ability level, the more greens a player could reach, the lower his score. The average male player (about an 18-handicap) is lucky to be on three greens each round. Double that figure and he'd be knocking on the door of 80.

The second factor, although much lower in impact than GIR, is distance, defined as the ability to score on long holes compared to shorter ones. According to Riccio, an improvement of 10 yards for the high-handicapper would help only about one shot a round. Obviously, if you hit so short that most par-4s are unreachable, you won't be able to score much better unless you can find some increase in distance. However, if you can hit 200 yards with a driver, distance is not a critical barrier to good scoring.

Very similar in effect to length—but much easier to improve—is reducing your number of awful hits. Statistically, the average golfer adds a half shot for every hack, top, or chili dip.

Fourth is iron accuracy. The average golfer hits the green with his iron shots about 3 times out of 20. Those who break 80 do it about 10 out of 20. This is a different notion than greens in regulation, for the shot counts even if it's the

10th or 11th swing on that hole, but the relationship between the two is easily seen. Working on hitting accurate irons is clearly a good use of practice time.

Equal to iron accuracy is putting—what many of us think of as the main scoring tool. What is instructive to note is that the average player putts about 36 times a round, the "regulation 2 putts per hole." If a professional putted for you, at the usual professional level of 29 putts per round, you'd still score in the 80s.

Because totaling putts per round mixes up missed greens and chipping ability, good chipping can make a mediocre putter look good, at least on paper. To better identify the real effect of putting, Riccio developed a concept called ProPutts, which compares the average number of putts a typical professional would take for a given length of first putts to what you take. For example, let's say that professionals average 1.85 strokes from 18 feet, and you take 2. Calculate this difference over 18 holes or more and your total number of putts can be compared to the experts'. This and other forms of adjusting for missed greens and chipping effects are necessary convolutions if we're to determine the true importance of putting.

Analyzing your own game should begin with simply counting how many greens you're able to reach in regulation then determining what you should improve to increase that number. For most of us, that means hitting irons a tad farther and a tad straighter, or maybe taking one more club. Then again, the solution may be buying a new set of graphite, perimeter-weighted, oversized, diamond-coated irons with extra-forgiving shafts and a strong loft angle . . . but probably not.

The range is the best place to improve your swing. You'll have enough time to sort out the problem and enough balls to prove the solution. Trying something out for the first time while playing is usually doomed to failure no matter how appropriate the change.

6

PLAYING THE GAME

Love

It's easy to understand how golf can be a love affair, but not so easy to know when it has become something more akin to a fatal attraction. Many private clubs have a member or two whose bags no longer contain a full set of clubs. Some of these curmudgeons spend hours observing the course through binoculars, calling the pro shop whenever a stranger walks the fairways or a member is about to take illegal relief. Others man committees, almost with helmet and gun, as if civilization itself will collapse unless the bunker on five is kept exactly where it is. There is an invisible line between love and obsession, just as there is between dedication and obnoxiousness. Our passion should encourage others to cherish our great pastime, not drown their interest in a flood of rules and regulations.

It's a given that many love the game. And because the opposite of love is indifference, wise golfers accept that playing the game also includes hate, despair, irritation, and a host of other unpleasant feelings. Love also stimulates silliness and a good deal of what looks to outsiders like obsessive behavior. But that's golf.

A small group of golfers meets now and then at St. Andrews during the long days of summer (much of Scotland is at the same latitude as southern Alaska, and thus enjoys similar twilight). They call themselves the International Eight to Eights, occasionally captained by Martin Farrally of the university. This ragtag bunch gathers on the first tee of one of the town's courses and tees off at the stroke of 8 P.M. They play 18 holes that evening and retire, either to the nearest pub or to bed. They gather again at dawn to get in a second 18 before 8 A.M. Anyone is welcome to join this group: Just show up, declare yourself, and play. The larger the gathering, the more sweet tension will arise as the last groups of the morning hurry to finish before the stroke of 8. Failure is an automatic invitation to try again the next evening.

Some players take pride in having played 72 holes in a day, 14 rounds in a week, or 3,000 different courses in a lifetime. Collectors abound. Matty Reed owns something like 50,000 golf clubs (that's right). Mark Sukerman has perhaps 2,000 different scorecards. Bob Smith can show you 30,000 golf balls. And if you want golf facts, John Gleason has been collecting them since 1954, and what's amazing is that these thousands and thousands of facts are all neatly filed in his Florida home for easy access. He has over 800 books and many times that number of newspaper clippings. He's going to write a book himself as soon as he gets caught up with his filing.

Teams of golfers spread out on a course to break the speed record, some using the same ball on all the holes, others a new ball on each tee. (Each method has a separate record that's surprisingly quick—less time than it takes a foursome to play only a medium-length par-3.)

Jaunts by jet planes are designed to take you to courses on three different continents within 24 hours. A fortunate few collect all the courses on *Golf Digest*'s 100 best. Bob McCoy managed to play all of *Golf Magazine*'s top 100 golf courses in the world in 100 days (traveling 52,500 miles and walking every course). Many more travel a shorter distance to a venue played by tour professionals, traipse to the back tees, and tackle it like their heroes.

Indifference is the enemy, while love is the energy that must be channeled. Unless we care, and care deeply, golf is no more than a modicum of exercise and a series of half-hearted swipes at a little ball. At its best, the game swings us from agony to euphoria much the way a gorilla might fling about a doll. Golfers do strange and wonderful things under its spell. The evening after Tom Watson won the British Open at Muirfield, Ben Crenshaw somehow procured a set of ancient golf clubs and a gutta-percha ball and declared he would play at least two holes in the soft glow of twilight on the Firth of Forth. Tom Watson and both men's wives, Tom Weiskopf, Bill Rogers, Andy North, Bruce Lietzke, and Tony Jacklin made up the gallery. While Ben was busy making bogey on the first hole he played (the same score he made with modern equipment during the last round of the tournament), Linda Watson left and then returned with a piper in full Highland regalia. Caught up in the moment, Tom Watson challenged Ben and, bantering in the best Scottish accents they could muster, the men played a rousing one-hole match. Watson won with a putt from 7 feet. "A good match sir," Watson said, offering his hand to Crenshaw. "Aye," the Texan drawled, "a bonnie good match."

Golf is love: love of the challenge, the surroundings, the companionship, even the frustrations and disappointments. Those who know about the science of love* have divided this mysterious feeling into three components: commitment, passion, and intimacy. Golfers know these divisions well.

Commitment to the game is demonstrated by zealous club cleaning, purchase of foul-weather knee-high rubber boots complete with spikes, and waking up hours before dawn to get a good spot in the long line in front of the starter's booth.

There is passion. No one who loves the game was without tears as Ben Crenshaw bent from the waist and covered his face with his hands after sinking his last putt to win the Masters or as Arnold Palmer walked over the old stone bridge at St. Andrews and waved during his final appearance in the British Open. Many cried with Mark Calcavecchia as he sat sobbing on the beach after faltering in his Ryder Cup match. All walked with victorious Jack

---

*P. G. Wodehouse observed love and golf from this perspective: "What is love compared to holing out before your opponent?"

Nicklaus up the hill to the 18th green at Augusta that wonderful Sunday afternoon in April 1986. Few of us experience such intense golf experiences personally, but we can share them.

The 19th hole was invented as a roundtable for stories, an audience for expressions of joy, and a crisis response unit for near-terminal dejection. Intimacy is created when you listen to tales of woe and another listens to your story of high drama. Sharing thoughts and observations of life is almost a rule as two players walk, step matching step, down the fairway. It is a ritual of passage for parents to listen to blow-by-blow accounts of every shot when a child makes par, breaks 100, or finally climbs that highest of hills and finishes one up against old Dad.

Love means respect. For golfers, that's easy. Know the rules and obey them, even when it breaks your heart. Appreciate the course: Fix ball marks, repair divots, minimize noise pollution, don't dress like a clown. When you shoot an eight, write an 8 on the card. Take your turn keeping score, too. When it's your turn to hit, be ready. When holding the flagstick, rest the end on the toe of your shoe, not on the green's surface.

Love also means taking responsibility. Professionals talk about protecting the field. Tiger Woods won his second professional tournament when Lennie Clements blew the whistle on young Taylor Smith. It seems that Taylor finished even with Tiger, but did so using a long putter with a split grip. The rule for a split grip is that both grips have to be round; Taylor's weren't. Many observers were critical: Clements should have kept quiet about such a technicality, he should have told only Taylor, or he should have somehow noticed earlier and done something before the round.

The responsible player doesn't interpret the rules, but follows them. He doesn't follow them some of the time but all of the time when playing golf. Committees can interpret, modify, or eliminate rules as necessary—not players. The player who loves golf, plays golf and not a hybrid, unless a hit-and-giggle round is the intended game for the day.

A few years ago Paul Azinger ran into problems when he thoughtlessly moved some rocks with his feet while taking his stance in a hazard. A few pebbles was all. There was no intent to gain an advantage: he was just getting comfortable. Obviously, a couple of small stones is nothing. Neither, perhaps, are three slightly bigger ones. And heck, four or five is so close to just a couple as to be the same thing. And on and on. A responsible player accepts the rules of the game.

In an unusual circumstance—one that could only happen on the professional circuit—Tiger Woods found himself behind a boulder on the 13th hole during the 1999 Phoenix Open. But this was Tiger, followed by his usual overflowing gallery. Help was at hand. A full dozen of his fans struggled together to move the rock out of his way. A boulder! He went on to make birdie. The rulebook is clear: A loose impediment, any stone of any size—provided it is not embedded—may be removed by any means. In this instance the rules were to Tiger's advantage. Rules are rules, for good or ill, and ill is often the case. We should be glad when they can be used to move small mountains.

Perhaps the best example of ill being the case was Greg Norman's disqualification from a tournament because the name printed on his ball was not one of the names printed on the approved ball sheet. The ball was legal in weight, shape, size, and performance, but no name, no game. Any less is anarchy, or a game other than golf.

When you love golf, you'll experience a metamorphosis of the best kind. You'll transcend being merely a recreational participant. Almost every golfer has heard this story. Joe has had a miserable day: three triple bogeys, four quadruple bogeys, and the rest of his card was *really* bad. He lost 20 bucks six ways. He has had enough. After stumbling off the last green, Joe gives away his bag and clubs to his caddie and hides himself in a dark corner of the locker room. There he takes out a razor blade and slices both wrists. As the blood pours to the floor, his buddy Frank calls out from three rows away, "Hey Joe, wanna play next week?" Joe presses both wrists together to stop the bleeding and yells back, "What time?"

Even the legendary Babe Ruth had trouble giving up the game. "No more golf for me," he once said to a friend. "But I tell you . . . if you're not busy we could meet on the first tee tomorrow morning, because if I'm going to quit I might as well get in one more game."

Loving the game means saying you're sorry. You apologize to your partner. You promise to play a shot better during the round, fail to do so, call yourself every name in the book, eventually forgive yourself, and play on. You even apologize to yourself while driving home, vowing it will be different next time.

We can hate this game and we can hate ourselves as we play it but we'll be back. Hate is part of that passionate love that twists and torments. The elation of a well-played 3-wood to a par-5 green is brutally debased by taking three putts for par. Yet we come back. We come back because golf is the kind of game that evokes much more than simply enjoyment of an afternoon's sport. Our knee-jerk, self-indulgent tantrums are minuscule compared to the complex universal microcosm that is this game. Eventually we catch on to that.

Yet it is a sad golfer indeed who cannot justify flinging—at least once in a playing career—a recalcitrant club far into the nearest large body of water never to be seen again. Henry Longhurst made doing so a sensuous experience. "The most exquisitely satisfying act in the world of golf is that of throwing a club. The full backswing, the delayed wrist action, the flowing follow-through, followed by that unique whirring sound, reminiscent only of a passing flock of starlings, are without parallel in sport."

Enjoyment

If you're going to play the game, a simple truth is that you should always enjoy it. Given the nature of golf this might not seem so easy to do, but it is. A true golfer enjoys playing no matter what his score, the conditions, or the course, and that attitude should be obvious to everyone nearby. There are two ways to do this. The first is to make sure you learn something every time you play. The second is to return something to the game every time you play, too.

Naturally, playing golf with friends on a challenging course, on a warm spring day, and well within your handicap makes enjoying golf easy. It's those other days that take more effort. To enjoy golf no matter what the weather or score by learning something, it's useful to set a goal or two before play. These goals could be anything from appreciating the design features of a course you haven't played before to hitting too much club rather than not enough. Setting and achieving a goal separate from the score or outcome of a match feels good, and if the goal is defined well, it usually enhances play anyway.

To contribute each time you play is even easier. Fix your ball mark and one or two more. Pick up bits of stray trash, give a spare rulebook to one of the kids on the practice green, be especially courteous to the folks in the pro shop, take the starter a cup of coffee, wave to the lady on the mower. There's more. Rake the bunker if it needs it, even if you weren't in it. If it's breezy at all, hold the flag as well as the flagstick. Say a simple "thank you" if you're praised for a shot, and don't use more than two sentences describing it.

Don't complain. Don't whine. If you spot a problem, fix it, or make sure that someone who can fix it knows about it. Decide to do these things before you begin your game.

Serious players, those who have suffered at the crucible of competitive golf, are well aware that the game is a compendium of human experience. As such, golf can be an effective avenue to civic maturity. Golf teaches a kind of character that travels much farther than through the green. Raymond Floyd once said that if you could live life according to the rules of golf, you'd be living a pretty decent life. Living by the rules of golf means living a life of honor and fair play. This can be done, too, with a little conscious effort.

On the course, and everywhere else in life, learn to accept a bad lie. Admit mistakes. Have a target. Work to improve weak areas. Give the honor to one who has done better. Tempo. Balance. Rhythm. Harmony inside and out.

Extrapolate the simple acts of golf courtesy to the greater world around you. Standing so your shadow is not in your opponent's line elevates to donating a pint of blood to the Red Cross. Repairing someone else's ball mark is transformed into becoming your brother's keeper. The attitude of never wishing ill and always assuming your opponent will pull off a difficult shot keeps you sharp and acknowledges the worthiness of a competitor. Can this translate into global cooperation? Maybe.

Human Nature

The ego, Freud said almost 100 years ago, is besieged by three tyrants: the external world, the id, and the super-ego. Translated into English, this means that we are driven to go looking for trouble, and, once we find it, criticize ourselves for not knowing better.

Golf eventually humbles all who play it, which is why golf is a metaphor for life. It's also why we hate the game. The game and life, however, don't humble anyone. That's up to us to do to ourselves. On the first tee we take pride out of the bag at the same time that we pull out the driver.

If we didn't care, nothing would be important, and nothing would be attempted. Since we're driven to try, though, and to invest our egos in the result, our self-esteem is under constant attack—nowhere more so than on a golf course. The mature player understands that the game is infinitely stronger than the golfer. The less astute strut and crow after dropping a 10-foot birdie under the mistaken assumption that they have somehow brought the course to its knees.

"Golf," said P. G. Wodehouse through his character the Oldest Member, "acts as a corrective against sinful pride." He went on:

> I attribute the insane arrogance of the later Roman emperors almost entirely to the fact that, never having played golf, they never knew that strange chastening humility which is engendered by a topped chip shot. If Cleopatra had been ousted in the first round of the Ladies Singles, we should have heard a lot less of her proud imperiousness.

When Tiger Woods first burst onto the scene, the way his fist pumped with each winning putt was part of his "this guy is bigger than life" persona. Yet many letters to the editors of leading golf magazines compared his actions to the hip-swinging displays of arrogance on the football field or the increasingly disappointing behavior on basketball courts, tennis stadiums, baseball diamonds, and soccer pitches everywhere. Few in the civilized world enjoy the sight of a big defensive lineman pointing at and mocking a quarter-back he has just knocked down from the blind side. Golf is headed in the direction of other games, but it doesn't have to get there.

Golf, although perhaps a crueler game than others, remains one that can be played without expressing the baser levels of human nature. Ladies and gentlemen still play the game. Enjoyment of your achievements is fine; enjoyment at the expense of others isn't. Give a damn, do your best, and congratulate the winner on any given day, especially if the day has not gone well.

To protect ourselves from constant despair while on the links, we often apply the balm of psychological defense mechanisms. We blame everything but ourselves for a miss. We use a 4-iron to massage the ego when even our best 3-wood would come up short. We think our birdie, our disaster at the turn, our grasping victory on the 18th are the most interesting events history has witnessed and should be explained at length after the round to the assembled masses.

Golf is a humbling game and we either are forced or learn to be humble. It is a game of mistakes and we admit making them. Once we can accept playing in harmony with the realities of golf, our goal of always enjoying the game is achieved.

Fairness

Fairness is a hot issue these days, and, with golf's honor code still held in high regard, fairness is almost exclusively about golf-course setup. A notable example is the 1999 British Open at Carnoustie. Players said it was "over the top." The fairways were very narrow—so much so that a ball hit straight down one side easily could and did bounce and roll into the rough on the other side. The rough was thick, ankle-deep and deeper, making recovery shots akin to survival shots. Had the weather been any worse (wind of 35 mph or so the first day), none of the best players in the world would have broken 90. As it was, Sergio Garcia shot an 89 the first day and Jim Furyk declared, "That was the most demanding major—not even close. I've never played in a tournament before where 10 over par was a pretty good score." The R&A staunchly defended the layout. This small squabble highlights the complexity of what fairness really is.

Fairness can be a number of things: reward matching effort, equality, randomness, consistency, and so on: with consistency one of the more interesting elements when it is applied to golf.

All games require consistency; most provide it in the form of the playing field, rules, and equipment. It would do no good to have tennis courts of varying size and shape or with net heights ranging from 1 to 9 feet.

However, all games require inconsistency—otherwise players would be bored and the outcome wouldn't matter. For example, a baseball pitcher creates inconsistency by mixing up fastballs and curves to confuse the batter.

Similarly, a football quarterback calls different plays to confuse the defense; there are varied plays in soccer and basketball, even fake spikes in volleyball, to create inconsistencies that exploit either a weakness in the opposition or the strengths of your own team.

Sport demands inconsistency to create competition. The greater the difference between the game's consistency and its inconsistency, the more interesting the sport. An extreme example is the archaic sport of dueling. Consistency was in the ritualistic set of rules, inconsistency in the nerves of the combatants and the range of possible outcomes.

This leads us to the question of what should be consistent and inconsistent in golf. The possible variables are rules, players, weather, equipment, and courses. I'll assume that the rules will remain as consistent as they have for the last 100 years and will be followed equally well. And I'll have to assume that the weather will be inconsistent. But golf, or any game, would be worthless if the weather was the only element of surprise or challenge. (Around-the-world sailing races like the Whitbread are the exceptions—but they wouldn't be if, during extreme conditions, everyone could retire to the clubhouse for a cup of tea.) Golfers, although unique individuals, have one consistent goal: to take the fewest strokes possible. Although team play adds one variable, this is not as important an area of inconsistency in golf as it is in other sports, where team members have varied positions and assignments.

Club manufacturers would like us to believe that there is significant variability among clubs, with their particular brand superior to the others. The USGA and R&A, meanwhile, are doing their best to ensure that equipment remains as consistent as possible—so that a good shot is the result of skill rather than engineering. It does not take a genius to understand the need for equipment to remain what it always has been, a tool dependent on the ability of the player.

It seems clear that for golf to be golf, and to be an enjoyable and challenging game, there must be inconsistency in the playing field, exactly the opposite of most games. The only question is, How much inconsistency is fair?

If golf is a game played out in the open in a natural setting, then the more natural—and thus the more random the inconsistency—the fairer the course. *Fair* is random inconsistency, what nature provides—what golf was in the old days.

However, when courses are created by professional designers, maintained by college-trained superintendents, and played by those who expect something other than randomness, the game becomes vulnerable to complaints of "this course is unfair."

Nothing could be less valid. Since designers will always come up short of the inconsistencies nature can provide, the best that can be done is to create an interesting test. The more designers try to manipulate a site into a golf course, the more likely the layout will seem artificial or contrived and by degrees be declared "unfair." It is still a golf course of relative value, however.

Anyone who complains that golf is an unfair game probably hasn't played it. Anyone who says a golf course is unfair just doesn't get it. A course can be many things: short, long, tough, easy, in bad shape, poorly set up, badly designed. But *fair* is not, nor should it be, a word used to describe a golf course—which is of necessity inconsistent. The course, like the universe, just is, and you play it as you find it.

Handicaps

Donald Trump, he of the megadeals and megatowers, has a very low one—some say too low. Superbillionaire Bill Gates has a high one—some say too high. The average (around 17 or 18) hasn't changed much in two decades. It is a source of pride, despair, a sign of aging, a symbol of passing the torch, and a passport to the golfing world.

It is one of golf's greatest inventions, enabling one person to compete fairly against someone else of considerably different skill. You can compete on the same playing field as the best professionals, something you can't enjoy in any other sport. Ideally, and everything being equal, handicaps should promote competition so that the outcome is uncertain until the last hole, no player given advantage over another except by good play.

Handicaps have been around for more than a century, the first effort being the informal giving and taking of stokes during match-play competition. As club meetings became more popular, a method of equating many players was established, and improvements have been made continually ever since. There are many systems to consider. Your handicap, for example, could be based on your last 10 scores, throwing out the best and worst and dividing by 8; or you could add up points, two for eagle, three for birdie, four for par, and so on. However it is done, the idea is to give everyone an equal opportunity for success.

The elements involved in creating a good handicap system are complex. Somehow, all the differences in golf courses have to be equated. The par-5 18th at Pebble Beach is a far different hole from the par-5 18th at Torrey Pines. The myriad golfing skills within each player have to be quantified to somehow be productively compared to everyone else. Can someone who is a good chipper and putter but cannot hit long irons be fairly compared to someone who belts the ball a mile, can't chip, but is a deadly putter? Other realities have to be factored in, including the wide range of scores possible from the high-handicapper, the difference between one-stroke improvement possibilities of low- and high-handicap players, and how one golfer can earn his handicap with consistent scores and another with great variation. Finally, different types of competition require different types of handicapping. Somehow course, golfer, and game factors have to be defined, measured, computed, tested, and constructed into a system that would work on the first tee of courses around the world.

For medal events, a handicap that emphasizes a player's best scores (like taking the best 10 scores out of 20) provides the most level playing field. For match play, however, using some sort of average of every round seems to work well. But if a large number of scores is put into simulated playing situations—as the USGA has done—and multiple handicaps are evaluated for producing fair outcomes, the one that proves best under most conditions is the current USGA slope system. It is actually quite elegant.

This is how it works. Trained raters walk a course to measure 10 factors on a scale of 0 to 10. The factors are: topography, fairway, recoverability and rough, out of bounds, water hazards, trees, bunkers, green target, green surface, and psychological factors. Also taken into account are length, roll, prevailing wind, elevation, altitude, and hole shapes. A course rating is established, which is independent of par and can be equal to, higher than, or lower than the par for the course. This number is the real expected score for the expert golfer. From this rating, the factors are weighed in two ways, for the expert player and for the bogey golfer. This is where the slope concept comes in. The greater the difference in the rating between the expert and the bogey player, the steeper (higher) the slope rating.*

Before this system, all courses were rated for the scratch golfer, and all golfers were compared to the scratch player. Now all you have to do to carry a usable handicap from course to course is to have a USGA handicap index and look up the slope chart of the course you're playing to determine that day's handicap. It will be lower if the course is easier for your ability level; higher if the course is more difficult. (This works because the chart multiplies your index by the course's slope and divides by 113, rounding off to the nearest whole number.) Research has shown that the great majority of courses, golfers, and games fit nicely into this statistical method.

But because golf mimics life, some players don't fit the system, by choice. Every course has its sandbaggers. Even a couple of PGA pro-am tournaments have been tarnished by the odor of flatulent handicaps. At the AT&T Pebble Beach National Pro-Am not long ago an amateur teamed with a professional to take the top prize. The amateur produced 45 of the duos' winning shots based on his 15 handicap. Trouble was, his handicap was from a club he owns. His real handicap was reputed to be 6. Tournament officials later disqualified the team, but allowed the pro to keep his $7,000 winnings when he was cleared of any duplicity.

In times past players wrote their scores on big sheets hung in a prominent place in the clubhouse—out in the open for all to see. If Smith was seen on the course five times one week but posted only one score, everybody knew about it. Nowadays most posting is done at a computer terminal, spawning privacy, confidentiality, and possibly petty

---

*For the more mathematically inclined, the slope is the regression line of total score versus handicap for a particular course. If the Y intercept is the course rating, the slope of the average course is equal to 1.13 (which is converted to 113 in order to use whole numbers). To use this as a reference for all courses, the slope rating of any course is found by multiplying the difference between the bogey rating and the course rating by a constant of 5.381.

larceny. Somehow writing scores in pencil on a public form is more conducive to full confession than a quick push of a couple of buttons. Handicaps, ego driven as they are, can demand more character than some people can supply.

The USGA has studied this problem for almost 25 years. First off it found that scores are not symmetrical; poor scores are more frequent for any player than good scores when compared to his average. This is one reason that handicaps are based on better scores rather than all scores. The question, though, is when is a good score suspiciously too good?

With all the USGA's statistics, any player's one-day score can be computed on a probability scale. More than 20,000 rounds have been studied from every angle. Probability can be determined almost to a certainty. A few winning net scores have been close to the million-to-one category. One miracle round, of course, should be congratulated. Two miracle rounds during the same tournament stretches credulity. Three or more should be viewed with sadness. These players have missed something along the way.

The USGA's decision is that if you have two or more unusually low tournament scores (at least three strokes lower than your handicap index), then the two lowest tournament-score differentials are computed (determining that day's "handicap"). This number is added to a predetermined "performance limit." This number, whatever it is, becomes your new handicap. You can fool the system only once.

Dean Knuth, a former USGA handicap expert, devised a way of identifying handicap cheats called the Knuth Tournament Point System. A player's success over two years is evaluated; anyone winning more than what is realistic can be given a more competitive handicap. His system, and more information about handicaps, can be found on his Web site (www.popeofslope.com).

Although handicaps can be distressing or be a source of pride, it is a wise and enlightened golfer who recognizes the true purpose of an accurate handicap—to provide an exciting match from the first tee shot to the last putt.

The Golfer on the Golf Course

A golf course is designed to make the most—or perhaps that should be the least—of human nature. The male ego, for example, is one of the major hazards to be found on any layout. Although the essence of golf is to accept the limits of your game, the majority of players are unwilling to agree with reality, even as shot after shot falls short of the target and into one or another sort of difficulty. All a golf course has to do is present the hole and allow human nature to rush into trouble.

Small children are well known for a belief system that is almost impervious to contradictory new information. Tell trusting kids that there's a rabbit in a box, leave them to think about that for a while, then open the box to show them that no rabbit is there. Many will insist they heard it and wonder where it went. Golfers are always trying to find that rabbit.

Take, for example, otherwise good golfers at the beautiful 16th at Cypress Point. Veteran professional Porky Oliver was easily able to carry the 233 yards to the green. Taking into account the yardage, wind, and probable bounce, he took his swing, connected well, and watched his ball bounce around the rocks below the green and then drop into the rolling water of the Pacific. Trusting his assessment of the shot more than the reality of the ball in the drink, he used the same club again with the same result. Twice more he relied on his belief and twice more his ball fell into the ocean. Worse was Henry Ranson's effort on the same hole. His ball landed on the beach, where his belief system inspired a recovery attempt from the sand. Belief won over reality 16 times before he finally picked up.

It's not only short holes that are unbelievable to the earnest player. The legendary Tommy Armour decided that one particular par-4 at the Shawnee Open required a drive down the right side of the fairway with a gentle draw back to the middle. His concept was finally proved after 10 tee shots went out of bounds. The even more legendary Arnold Palmer put five balls out of bounds on the ninth hole during the second round of the L.A. Open one year. When asked later how he had managed a 12 on such a relatively easy hole, he replied, "I missed my putt for an 11."

Then of course, golf being golf, the opposite is true. We can anticipate what might come true and make it happen. Look at the experience of many golfers playing the first hole on the East Course at Warren Valley just outside Detroit. In front of the tee meanders a small, slow-moving tributary of the Rouge River. The tee is elevated, and the width of the brown water is such that anyone over the age of six could throw a ball safely across. On average, however, three out of a foursome tee up water balls, and at least one player will lose it. Golfers can ignore reality and create it. It's hardly fair that the golf course presents challenges when so often the golfer's brain is a victim of its own thought process. But golf being golf, the playing ground is a minefield of danger, imagined and real.

There are four types of courses: the old-style penal courses, where a bad shot is severely punished; the strategic, where you can gain an advantage by playing smart shots; the heroic, where taking a risk provides clear rewards; and the resort style, at which golfers on a holiday play a beautiful course to take home a scorecard full of especially low or unusually high scores.

Since the basic idea of course management is to advance the ball to a better place, the course architect does everything he can to make that more of a challenge—by testing your strength, accuracy, wisdom, or (more likely) a crafty combination of all three. Take the sneaky arrangement of an easy par-4 followed by a difficult par-4. The easy par-4 might look that way because it's short. But if you unwarily play a driver in hopes of a quick three, you might find yourself bouncing into a pot bunker 30 yards short of the green; perhaps ending up with a hard-earned par or even bogey. You then must face the tough par-4 while still disgusted at the one that got away. You might add two or three shots to your card because of poor club selection on the easy hole and an inability to fully concentrate on the next. The course and human nature at their golfing best.

It's commonly accepted that a good golf course will create interest for all levels of players. Where modern courses have gone wrong is in trying to create equity between the shot and the result. That is, a shot that's 80 percent good should result in consequences that are 80 percent good, too. Despite statements to the contrary, the expectation of modern players is that the game will be fair, which pressures designers to produce bland courses or leads to frustrated golfers who don't understand the nature of the game. In the early 1930s H. N. Wethered believed that "the perfect shot is invariably rewarded; it is only right that the shot which is slightly imperfect should be weighed on the scales of providence."

Think of the joy players had in the old days when there were no real fairways—when the best way to the hole was decided individually by each player depending on skill, pluck, the weather, and the rub of the green. A bit of this can still be experienced today by anyone lucky enough to play a course backward. Or by playing sideways or any which way, choosing a green 400 or 500 yards away and hitting cross country. What fun this is, and how sad we have become, hitting down green bowling alleys and throwing darts at the hole instead of guessing which route around a knob in front of our target will produce the best results. Try cross-country golf sometime and see if you don't agree.

Another factor in course management is your shot-making ability. Hitting a lot of greens is of little use if you lag-chip better than you lag-putt. Nor is it smart to force a shot to a well-bunkered green if your sand play isn't very good.

Even more unwise is to take the driver out of your bag when the fairways are narrow and missing them could be a disaster. Distance isn't all that important. Next time you play, use just your 7-iron on a couple of holes until you get close to the green. You may be surprised at how well you score. Or play in a John Daly or Tiger Woods tournament. Under this format, whenever you hit a tee shot into the fairway, you're allowed to move the ball to where these boomers would land. Another surprise: Scores aren't that much lower.

Once you accept personal limitations, course management turns into figuring out how to minimize errors, mental and physical. The tasks you face with every shot are assessing what you must accomplish given the situation, identifying your shot options, comparing them to your ability to make them, then picking the one that has the best chance of success.

Say you're on the 18th tee at Pebble Beach, the 548-yard par-5 hard around the rock-bound waters of Carmel Bay. Would you automatically pull a driver out of the bag? Your first question is: What's the situation? Need eagle to make the cut? Bogey to win the tournament? A halve to win the match? The concept to know is how much you need, how much you're willing to risk, and how much is smart to risk. Often these are three different things.

If you have a five-shot lead on the field, the prudent play would be a series of 7-irons until the green was well within range. Not many competitors would have the self-assurance to play it that way, however, given the risk of scorn from spectators and fellow competitors for such a cowardly approach. On the last hole of the 1999 British Open, for instance, Jean Van de Valde squandered a three-shot lead when a series of 7-irons would have won him the claret jug. Yet choosing too easy a shot, using far too much club, or picking a safe but unappealing route often does more harm than good. Concentration can wander or ambivalence ruin the swing.

Similarly, what looks like a mistake may, in fact, be good. A player who to the unaware foolishly chooses a driver may have much more confidence in that club than a balky 3-wood. This is good course management. John Daly won the British Open at St. Andrews by making a whole series of such useful errors.

At the same time, what feels good may be completely wrong, and what feels awkward might be just the ticket. An aggressive player like Greg Norman may feel very comfortable going for the pin or trying to make 40-foot putts, never realizing how many shots he's tossing away. Laying up on a reachable par-5 might feel like giving up a chance to putt for eagle and half stroke to the field. In essence, however, it may provide the best scoring average over four days of play. Two birdies and two pars beat an eagle, a birdie, and two double bogeys any day, especially when coupled with the emotional letdown of high scores on an easy hole.

Those playing the 18th at Pebble Beach—one of the best-finishing holes in golf—for the first time often will not play safe. Just as stubbornly, the great majority would not lay up on the par-3 16th a few miles away at the Cypress Point Club, or (in more mundane circumstances) play a wood when others are hitting irons. The urge to play the hole "right" sometimes becomes irresistible.

Your perception of the hole is another hurdle, for so much of a golf hole's difficulty is in how you look at it. Even such a simple view as either liking or disliking a hole, course, or tournament makes a big difference in your approach and your ability to play well. This is, perhaps, why eminent ball striker Lee Trevino never won the Masters.

As for the physical layout of a hole, you have the cunning of the architect to contend with. The architect's job is to interest you, get you involved, challenge your ability, make you sweat just a bit. Noted designer A. W. Tillinghast has this to say:

> A round of golf should present 18 inspirations—not necessarily thrills, because spectacular holes may be sadly overdone. Every hole may be constructed to provide charm without being obtrusive about it.

Modern architect and critic Tom Doak has strong feelings about recent trends in hole design and the resultant decline of golf. He believes that "the golf course with the widest variety of holes has everything." It will be fair because it's not biased for one particular type of shot. It will be balanced by variety. It will flow rather than plod, find the wind from all points of the compass, delight the eye, and interest everyone. Bad courses, by contrast, are bulldozed into the architect's vision, reshaping natural features into a fanciful artificial playground. Doak goes on to explain:

> The science of golf may have come a long way in the last hundred years, but in many respects, these "improvements" have taken away from the art of shot making. Golf courses have become relatively standardized in their demands and hazards, and the science of golf course maintenance has advanced to the point that the golfer seldom encounters a bad lie in the fairway or bunker, or a bad bounce on his approach.

Maybe this is why course management has been relegated to the back pages of instruction books. Many players admit to playing more by personal style than by what might work best. Quite a few define themselves as "double-bogey-birdie-par-eagle" kinds of players.

At the same time, however, being true to yourself is also good course management no matter who the self or what the outcome. We cannot criticize Billy Joe Patton's attempt to reach Augusta's par-5 15th back in the 1954 Masters. The lunky amateur with the stylish crew cut surprised himself and everyone else with a hole-in-one during the last round to jump into contention against the steel-hard duo of Hogan and Snead. Patton kept gunning at every pin, eventually pulling even with Hogan and one ahead of Snead. On that fateful par-5 15th he dumped his second into the water, carded a seven, and eventually finished one stroke out of a Hogan-Snead playoff. "I didn't come to play safe," he said. No regrets.

Golf is a game, like chess, Monopoly, pick-up sticks, or any other form of play. It is not an activity that advances knowledge, feeds the poor, or finds a cure for disease. It's swinging a stick at a ball. John Daly dissected the Old Course at St. Andrews by attempting shots criticized by almost everyone. Jack Nicklaus, as a television commentator, told his audience over and over what club Daly should be using on each tee while Daly simply kept whaling away with his driver. There is no law against playing a heroic shot, even if it's with every swing. There is no right way to play a hole. You can analyze percentages and play like someone solving algebra problems or be driven by inner demons to bring the course to its knees or die trying. Neither is better or more correct.

Just as there is no best way to play a hole, there is also no best way to understand how to play it and what the results should be. Amateurs everywhere are happy to attempt a quiverful of heroic shots and need only a single bull's-eye or even a near-miss or two to make the day a success. Effective course management is being aware of the problems a hole presents and making a conscious decision about how to attack it, combined with a willingness to rethink your decision as conditions change. Effective course management is second-guessing after the round. Better players are always looking for ways to improve, and assessing decisions is one of the best. Serious players should monitor their games to improve decision making and be willing listeners as others recount a round. Likewise, good (in contrast to effective) course management is a willingness to risk and to accept the results, like Billy Joe Patton did.

Ultimately, course management is enjoying the day's play. This may be heresy for some, but the best reason to stand on the first tee is the sheer joy of being outdoors and hitting a ball out among the grass and sand and hills, and doing things you weren't quite sure you could do with people who appreciate the effort.

The Target

Here's a common bit of advice to the beginning novelist: "Begin the story at the very last moment possible and end it right after the greatest conflict is resolved." It should come as no surprise that the same advice holds true for a game as full of passion and heroic disaster as golf. Just as some writers begin a story too early and never seem to get to the end, golfers tend to become distracted and fail to correctly identify the desired outcome.

Here's a quick quiz on the idea. On a 10-foot putt, what's your primary goal? It's *not* sinking the putt. Even the best putter has less than a 50 percent chance of making a putt from 10 feet. Focusing on that kind of outcome is counterproductive and discouraging. Before attempting the putt, your goal should be a good read on the speed and break. After that, the goal is putting a good stroke on the ball. The next goal is knowing why the ball missed if it did. Your final goal is knowing how to hit the next putt after having observed what happened to the first.

The shorter the shot, by the way, the more specific the target and desired outcome. For most players, no matter what the shot, there should be no more than two objectives. For a tee shot your goals might be to finish the backswing and to land just short of the left-side bunker. An elegant and effective objective of this type is described in Kjell Enhager's book *Quantum Golf.* Here he advocates focusing on making a "superfluid swing" rather than making a par or hitting the ball as far as possible.

Your target should always be something within your control. A baseball player who wants to improve his hitting will not have as his goal an average of .330 or hitting 10 percent more singles. Neither of these is a target under his control. Instead, his target should be swinging at more good pitches or swinging on a more horizontal plane. He can do both no matter if it's the "Big Unit" or Mickey Mouse glaring down from the mound.

Can you appreciate the beauty of a well-hit 3-footer that rolls exactly where you intended, even if it doesn't go in the hole? Okay, this may be asking too much, but you get the idea.

Shot Making: You Can't Get There . . .

Dave Marr, a noted player and announcer, once described a player's situation as impossible. "There is no way he can reach the green from there," he said. After the ball flew below, up, and around a few trees to finally land near the pin, Dave acknowledged, "Well, that's why he's down there and I'm up here!" Maneuvering the ball at will elevates golf from a craft to an art and, by all accounts, defines a true golfer. I've already discussed how modern courses and clubs minimize working the ball; that is, perhaps, reason enough to encourage a resurgence of shot making. Physical chemist and philosopher Michael Polanyi tells us why we should care, and why it's getting late:

> An art which has fallen into disuse for the period of a generation is altogether lost. There are hundreds of examples of this to which the process of mechanization is continuously adding new ones. These losses are usually irretrievable. It is pathetic to watch the endless efforts—equipped with microscopy and chemistry, with mathematics and electronics—to reproduce a single violin of the kind the half-literate Stradivarius turned out as a matter of routine more than two hundred years ago.

Shot making isn't a dead art—yet. The nature of the game, even on the simplest of courses, still requires a half shot from off the green or a knock out from within trees.

We are, however, swiftly going in the wrong direction. To our eyes, a ball bounding up to the green and close to the flagstick is boring golf compared to a high-flying ball that lands 20 feet past and spins backward toward the hole. We have learned the new standard of one right way to the hole—that of straight shots in the air—and deem everything else to be poor stepchildren. That's too bad. Controlling the trajectory, distance, and curve of the ball separates the player from the golfer. Players should have a bit of the artist in them, that gift to see and do more than is apparent at first, and share it with others.

Imaginative shot making is in the top rank of what makes golf special, along with etiquette, the grand outdoors, and honest play. No other game allows the variety of problem solving that golf once offered, and should continue to.

Isn't it a delight to overcome a bad tee shot by hooking your approach around the spreading limbs of an oak tree? How about drilling a low liner under that same tree and up over the next one? Those who can do it just love watching the tee ball follow the curve of the fairway. The same players can also hit low screamers into the wind—shots that don't balloon halfway out and then come roaring back.

There are many circumstances in which being able to shape a shot pays substantial dividends. The player stuck with hitting only from left to right is in trouble when faced with a green that severely slopes that same way. His usual flight would likely slide right off the green, whereas a right-to-left spinner would probably land and stop. Trouble shots in particular often call for spinning the ball one way or another or lessening spin to good effect.

Unfortunately, and contrary to what the USGA's technical director Frank Thomas has to say, technology has done considerable damage by all but eliminating one of the great joys of play: maneuvering the ball by design. Because of the vastly improved and uniform conditions of courses where nothing but straight and high shots are required, the forgiveness built into every game-improvement club, and the spin and trajectory purchasable with every sleeve of balls, shot making has all but disappeared. It's harder to hit a hook or slice because clubs have been designed to minimize that effect, and it's hardly necessary anyway when 3-wood approach shots stick on the green like landing in mud. Modern courses ask only that you know how far away the target is (and help you do so by strewing yardage markers around the fairways), and modern clubs encourage only one shot.

A few tour players are comfortable fashioning shots during a tournament. Most can't. Few amateurs even think to try. Should you have familiarity with this archaic skill? Almost 100 years ago John Low (*Concerning Golf,* 1903) had this to say:

> Every fresh hole we play should teach us some new possibility of using our strokes and suggest to us a further step in the progress of our golfing knowledge.

Or, of course, we could do our best to hit all our shots straight and high, perhaps by purchasing the latest in high-tech equipment, and leave shot making to a few crusty old diehards who think it's fun.

The Art of Putting

Ben Hogan hated it, declaring he would be happy if it was abolished. Bob Jones was just average at it for a while. Bernard Langer knows a dozen ways to do it. Hale Irwin missed a 1-incher during the British Open. Gene Sarazen promoted doubling the size of the hole. It's the easiest and hardest stroke in the game. There is no right way to do it, but there are many wrong ways. Dave Pelz has made a science of it. Lee Trevino had the best advice: "Keep it low."

For all classes of golfer, the putter is the most used club in the game, even though top amateurs and professionals average less than 30 putts per round. The best make only half their efforts from 8 feet but are deadly from a yard in. Yet nowhere else on the course are players more equal than on the putting surface. And nowhere else is the task so clear and failure so obvious. Things are magnified on the green. A butterfly flapping by on its irregular path becomes a great winged pterodactyl. Blades of grass rise up like a sea of saguaro cactus. Unrepaired ball marks are as big as divots.

The ego enlarges, too. Greens are judged too hard, too fast, too slow, too bumpy, too large, or too slopey by those who wouldn't know a stimpmeter from a thermometer. "Greens aren't like this back home," they argue. Balls hit from 30 feet that graze the hole should have gone in, despite rolling 10 feet past. The edge of the cup is examined with steely eyes if a short one spins out. More putters are broken or abandoned than any other club. The average player knows he is a much better putter than his friends think he is.

Yet the ego deflates quickly, often as you set foot on the green. Putting is the culmination of everything that came before. Long, towering tee shots and approaches of laserlike accuracy are rendered superfluous by the smallest of twitches within a foot or two of the goal. Big, beefy men are reduced to quivering cowards when facing a slippery downhill 5-footer. A three-putt—or, horrors, a four-putt—can destroy a round and ruin a man. Putting is cruel. Make a long snake and you're lucky. Sink a tough one from 5 feet and all you're doing is what's expected of you. "The devoted golfer," Dan Jenkins says, "is an anguished soul who has learned a lot about putting just as an avalanche victim has learned a lot about snow."

Nowhere else in golf, however, is artistry more apparent than the stroke of a putt, the soft click, and the long running curve to the cup. This follows the craftsmanship of developing an eye for the slope and the speed of the grass. Learning to read grain is a lifelong task, mastered only by a few fortunate enough to grow up in the South where grain can make balls curl uphill. There is technique. Hold the club so your hands oppose one another. Stand so your eyes are over the ball. Don't ever break the left wrist. There is psychology and truth in the old adage that if you think you're a good putter or if you think you're a bad putter, you're right. And there is logic. When old pro Don Witt was asked by a student how to make more putts, he gruffly answered, "Hit the ball more at the hole."

Dave Pelz provides the science. In 1989 he reported the result of his experiments on sinking putts: The optimum average speed to overcome spike marks, footprints, and the like is that which puts the ball 17 inches past the hole if it happens to miss. Less and the chances of being knocked off line increase. More and the chances of lipouts increase. A few years later, after more experiments, he reported that most golfers underestimate how much break there is in a putt, misalign the clubface closer to the true line, then somehow compensate even more with the stroke. The end result is that we all tend to miss the majority of breaking putts on the low side. Pelz suggests getting behind the estimated aim line rather than the ball to figure the break. Sadly, one of his findings is that few golfers accurately read the green even after seeing the break of a similar putt.

The artistry of putting is not in the stroke. Form in putting often follows function. An ungainly short pop is favored by those who grew up on rough greens, while the more attractive and graceful long stroke is popular for smoother, faster surfaces. Nor is artistry in the stance, like judging ballet positions for form and balance. Whether it's a Palmer knock-knee or a Raymond Floyd feet-together upright, stance is what works. Artistry isn't even in the results. Like all art, it is in the joy of the doing.

Putting is not the last barrier to a good score, it's a brush stroke on a green canvas. The ball, clean and white, wishes to run to the hole urged by the touch of the master. Gravity, your opponent until now, has become your ally. Uphill you can rap with authority. Downhill the ball must run to the hole and nowhere else. There is no trickery or deceit. All putts are straight.

The terror of putting comes from unrealistically expecting the ball to go in the hole. The yips (an uncontrollable flinch) occur when the focus is on the likelihood of missing and the consequent and legitimate fear of making the stroke. Tension builds in the shoulders and forearms to the point that you lose muscle control. No one wants to stroke the ball knowing the result will be disaster. Remove your ego from the result and invest it in the stroke. Focus on following through to your target. If you're going to miss, miss beautifully.

Strategy 201

One of the agonies of golf is that there is no defense. In a match or a tournament you have no control over your fellow competitors. Standing on the green with your hands in your pockets and helplessly watching your opponent crouch over a makable winning putt is akin to waiting to meet your daughter's fiancé for the first time. Yet few players grasp the idea that since there is no defense, golf is always a game of offense. You can't blacken the eye of an opponent or wrestle him to the ground, but you can and should attack the course with every shot. Rarely, however, with all guns blazing.

In the beginning, when golf was played over public land, there were as many ways to approach the green as there were players. Between tee and green were bumps, pits, and gorse. There was no paved highway of closely mown grass, but subtle wynds and sanctuaries visible to experienced players led eventually to the green and ultimately to the pin. The bump and run to the hole was the norm, banking the ball off one hill and rolling it over another. Attacking the hole was a well-planned campaign. With the air game played today, offensive golf has become a series of Hail Mary swings. Better golfers do it differently. A case in point: In the 1959 U.S. Open at Winged Foot, Billy Casper laid up all four days on a par-3, the tough 216-yard third hole. An unusual, even bizarre strategy. Other players went for the green, challenging the 100-foot-deep target, the bunkers on either side, and a very fast putting surface. Mr. Casper's technique allowed him to par all four days (and, incidentally, win the Open).

Good golf is not maximum distance but effective distance. Expert players call this the "risk-reward" decision. Before every shot you must ask yourself, "How much do I need, what options do I have, and how much am I willing to risk?" Every shot entails risk, and every shot must be chosen based upon a reasonable risk-reward analysis. There is, however, a catch.

Most football fans are familiar with the so-called prevent defense used during the final moments of a close game. The defensive team tries to avoid giving up a touchdown by allowing the offense to make short yardage but not the big play for a quick score. Too often, however, these short plays add up to a touchdown anyway.

The same holds true for golf. Playing safe is often unsuccessful. If par is needed on an easy par-4 hole, many golfers choose to hit the easiest tee shot. It's simple and safe, but often of little or no benefit. Take the case of poor David Ayton, who led the 1885 British Open by five strokes with only the Road hole and the last yet to play. Playing safe, he hit his approach to the 17th green short, leaving a run up to the flag. Playing safe again, he hit his bump and run too gently and the ball, losing speed, rolled off the green, stopping in front of the deep bunker on the left. Facing him was one of the most difficult shots in golf: pitching over the Road bunker, hard enough to get over but not so hard as to roll over the green onto the road—and this was for the championship. He hit too hard and the ball made the road. Ayton was running out of safety margin, but he did not want to hit the ball too hard from the road and end up in the Road bunker. He hit his next shot too soft and it didn't make it up the slope to the green. Instead, it rolled back onto the road. Naturally he hit the next shot too hard and ended up where he didn't want to be, the bunker. His first bunker shot was too soft. His second also stayed in the sand. One more effort put him on the green, where after two putts he was finally in, with an 11 on the par-4. He lost the championship by two strokes.

Playing safe by choosing the safest shot is not playing safe. No matter what the situation, attack everything that the defense—the golf course—will allow. This does not mean the easiest or safest shot, but the most offensive safe shot that the hole will give you. Golf is always offense, never defense. You are not trying to stop the course from scoring, but to score yourself.

Course Management

A well-designed course presents itself to the wise player, at least the second time around. Thinking like a wise player is a little more difficult. Take, for example, the way many otherwise excellent players approach that diabolical Road hole on the Old Course at St. Andrews. At over 460 yards, it's a difficult par-4 and, as you have seen, the site of disasters of historic proportion. That simple number, 4, is part of what fools many players. Par-4 theoretically means a tee shot, an approach, and two putts; therefore "reaching in regulation" requires being on the green with your second shot. That's what par-4 signifies to the golfer who isn't thinking. Bob Jones, the quintessential intelligent golfer, played the Road hole by hitting his second to a hollow just short of the green. He then chipped on and did his best to one-putt.

There are two conceptual traps to avoid. *In regulation* is the first. There is no official regulation written anywhere that a par-4 green must be reached with the second shot (take a hint from Jones), just as a par-3 doesn't have to be reached in one (and another hint from Casper) or a par-5 in three (pay no attention to Tiger Woods). *In regulation* is better understood as a design or statistical term. Holes can be one-shot, two-shot, or three-shot holes on the drawing board. As a statistic, your percentage of holes reached in regulation is a very good measure of your ability to score. Why should be fairly obvious. The more often the ball is on the putting surface, the more likely the next shot is to be a relatively simple putt. Simple, that is, when compared to the ball sitting in a bunker, the rough, within or near bushes or trees, up, down, or sideways on severe slopes, or in the pond in front of the green.

The second conceptual trap is the word *par*. No hole is constantly a perfect par-3, -4, or -5. Par is relative, depending on the inherent difficulty of the hole and the conditions you face while playing it. Ben Crenshaw, by the way, says that "the reason why the Road hole is the greatest par-4 in the world is because it's a par-5." Against a gale wind it might even be a par-6. Every hole actually has three pars: the one on the scorecard, the one determined by the hole's design and the day's conditions, and the one that exists for each player after every shot. If *par* is defined as the score an expert can expect to make on a hole, after a tee shot out of bounds even the best player may be able to expect only a double bogey. Thus, a poor tee shot might turn a par-4 into a momentary par-4.6. A subsequent good approach could change it to 3.3.

Professional golfers are especially susceptible to par pressure. The moans and howls are deafening if a hole appears tricky or unfair. Par-4s that mandate layups off the tee, fairways too narrow in the landing area, par-5s converted to -4s for major championships, and bumpy greens are all causes for considerable consternation. Only the best recognize that the hole plays the same for everyone. Only the best make the mental adjustment that par is an imaginary number that is always changing. The par of a hole is only a number, and of very little value except to the course architect, who hopes the numbers add up to 72. The concept of par is of no value in course management.

What *is* of value is knowing your own game and recognizing opportunity when it presents itself. The first rule of good course management has nothing to do with the course. Simply put, you must know and accept your limitations. This includes the real distance you normally hit each club and your usual flight pattern. Nothing defines the average golfer more than a tendency to come up short.

Sometimes bad course management is due to faulty analysis of the problem, failing to manage that 6-inch course between the ears, or believing course management isn't all that important. What constitutes golf today is the slash-and-burn mentality of a driver off every tee and irons at every flag. Somehow a smart layup has become unmanly. Heroic shots should always have a place, but so should patience and good judgment. Golf will cease to be a great game the moment brawn becomes more valued than thought.

Greg Norman was the number one player in the Sony world rankings in 1996. Yet in an early-1997 *Golf Digest* article he was criticized for poor course management, especially during his free-fall at the Masters. Former tour pro Jack Newton put it bluntly: "The biggest flaw in his game is course management. The bottom line is, it sucks."

In contrast is the approach of Jack Nicklaus. Major tournaments, Nicklaus always thought, were made easier to win because so many players could not withstand the pressure, played dumb shots, and thus took themselves out of it. It was also his thinking that par on any hole during a major championship was a good score. Norman and other swashbucklers like him have a hard time keeping their natural aggressive tendencies in check. If someone with the talent of Greg Norman has trouble here, all golfers should take a good look at themselves and where the game may be headed. If the importance of course management is diluted in favor of uniform courses, air golf, power golf, or easier courses that popularize the game, we've made a grave mistake. Golf is a game of uncertainty—in the player, in the design of the course, and in the bounce of the ball.

7

YOUNG PLAYERS

Knowledge

$\mathbf{A}$ t 7:30 sharp on a bright sunny morning two large, empty, but brightly decorated yellow school buses wind their way down Country Club Drive toward the city. It is Saturday, midsummer, and school has been out for more than a month.

At the same time, at the youth center in the heart of town, 60 scruffy kids ranging in age from 11 to 15 are beginning to gather. They have been anxiously waiting for three weeks, which seemed like years, for this day to arrive. During the long wait they took classes to learn when to be quiet, how to carry a bag, how to rake the sand, and how to hold the flagstick. Each passed a test, and this morning all are sitting at long tables having breakfast together, chatting with each other, wondering what the country club up on the hill will be like.

They hear the bus before they see it. Five dozen kids rush to get the best seats, the adults watching in amusement. The front four rows are reserved for them.

The annual Kings and Queens Tournament has a new twist this year: Princes and princesses have been invited. Sixty new members of royalty will be spread around the course in a shotgun start. They will carry bags, be served a lunch of burgers and hot dogs, and most will be invited back.

Eleven-year-old Tommy has a physics lesson on the fourth tee. Dr. Morgan's 4-iron shot was supposed to be his usual gentle fade 160 yards to the green. Instead, his ball almost circles the green from left to right, and ends up in the trees, clunking off three or four of them before it lands with a soft thump in the middle of a blackberry bush.

Tommy laughs, then notices Dr. Morgan's expression. "Oh, man. How did that happen?" the young man quickly asks, eyes wide in amazement.

King Morgan takes Prince Tommy aside. "The ball curved like that because it had spin on it, like a curveball in baseball."

"Wow." Tommy is impressed.

"Want to know how I did it?" Dr. Morgan can't control it, but the thoracic surgeon can slice with the best, and he knows why it happened. He explains two ball-flight laws to Tommy, using his 4-iron and another ball as visual aids. Tommy and the doctor have a great time together.

Entry fees went to pay for the buses, three weeks of classes at the youth center, and lunch at the club under the big red canopy set up just for junior royalty. Caddie fees were paid, and quite a few tips were well earned. Junior Golf donated clubs and balls for later use. The local driving range kicked in coupons and the promise of future help.

Two weeks later Tommy is using the first of his four passes to the driving range to see if he can hit the ball with spin, too. He has already amazed his mother by explaining elasticity and the rebound effect at the dinner table. Tommy's knowledge of golf is minimal but significant. He is beginning a lifelong adventure.

There are many kinds of golf knowledge. Dr. Morgan knew only a bit about the swing itself yet quite a lot about the human side of the game. Tommy became aware of its magic and wonder—and a little of its social rules, too. Golf is among the rare games today that require individual responsibility. Other games teach different values, while our cultural point of view seems to be slipping, too. Good information is part of the solution.

Knowledge is an understanding of a subject, and often with far-reaching implications. The better you understand something, the more you tend to respect it. With knowledge comes more than respect, however: There is also growing interest. Solving a difficult puzzle only makes you want to attempt another one. You have new confidence and, with it, greater enjoyment. With knowledge comes awareness of possibilities good and bad, of difficulty, of your ability to succeed, and of what is still unknown. Knowledge also provides well-defined goals and benchmarks for improvement. Acquiring knowledge and instilling it in others is perhaps the most important responsibility for anyone who loves the game.

As golf becomes more popular, knowledge will be diluted, fads will become facts, and guesses will become standards. New players, kids especially, should benefit from the best we can offer.

The Game of a Lifetime

A person's attitude to golf "is subconsciously conditioned for a lifetime by the circumstances in which one is first introduced to it," says golf writer and commentator emeritus Henry Longhurst. Those who hope to be good teachers should ensure that every student experiences golf at its best, holds the game in high esteem, and knows without doubt that it is a game to be cherished.

In the measureless reaches of the cosmos golf is hardly a ripple; it's a simple game of hitting a ball around an open field for a few hours of recreation. Only by keeping its traditions and investing in its future does it become more. What it becomes is up to us, each one of us, as we teach those new to the game and inspire those who don't yet understand. The next 500 years begin now, with you.

You may find some of golf's future lounging in your living room, or playing outside, or tapping on the keyboard of a computer upstairs. There may be grandchildren to teach, neighbors, Junior Golf players, or underprivileged kids needing a boost and new experiences. We all have a profound responsibility to introduce children to the game, and to do it well.

Golf is an easy game to learn if you learn it as a child and have childlike expectations. It is next to impossible to learn if you are a child and have the heavy hand of an adult pushing at your back or a hundred words of advice ringing in your ears. Guide the natural desire of children to explore new things and avoid dampening their spirits with a truckload of advice.

Golf is the game of a lifetime. There is no hurry to have your children develop the skill to knock a chip stone-dead to the hole or become the next Tiger Woods. You want them to love the game as you do. Before you do any teaching, reflect on what you love about golf. It is not just the ability to hit a shot that flies exactly as you planned, nor is it winning a hole or even shooting your best round ever. Your love of the game comes from enjoying the play and the companionship, coping with the unexpected, and feeling that occasional sense of mastery. You can help your kids experience the same things, which don't come from seeking perfection at each point in the swing, nor from following your instructions to the letter.

Let your children swing wildly, with a split grip and a reverse weight shift. Let them chop away like a lumberjack, spin around the left heel, or tap at the ball as if it were a soft-boiled egg. You want your kids to smile and say "thanks, that was fun" as they skip and hop away, excited about going out again.

Helping the next generation learn the game is an honorable effort and one heaped with danger. Many kids give up because learning golf is too frustrating and too hard, usually because an adult has made it so. The adult takes away the fun. Part of the problem lies in our expectations. Another is often inadequate or inaccurate knowledge and teaching skill.

The age of children is not important except as it relates to what they can learn. As soon as your kids express an interest in golf, it's time to start. The basic rule of thumb is that the younger the children, the less emphasis on teaching and the more on fun. At no age should enjoyment be less than the majority of the goal.

Your jobs are to identify the appropriate skills for your kids and to help them enjoy the learning process.

You don't have to be a good golfer yourself to teach your children well. You must, however, avoid teaching them bad habits. Many adults can play a good game despite bad swings because they have developed compensations for a bad grip or managed to deny reality sufficiently to believe their banana slice is a Hogan fade. Teaching your kids what works for you might not be doing them a favor.

Since it is impossible to define children's strength, coordination, motivation, and maturity by age alone, judge what and how to teach by their interest and ability to perform. There are no concrete standards as to the age at which kids should be able to swing well.

Avoid teaching too much—the most common error by far. This should be what happens at each golf lesson (and remember, not every golf outing should be a lesson):

1. The children enjoy the outing.
2. They perform much of what they've learned before.
3. They learn one new thing.

Do not go on to number 2 unless number 1 has been achieved and will not be affected by number 2. Do not go on to 3 unless 2 is done. Do not go on to a number 4. Leave that to professional teachers. Even they tend to preach too much.

Just as the kids have priorities, you should have your own set, too.

These are good ones for the teacher. Since you are older and more mature, you have a greater number of goals. They should be in this order:

1. Enjoy teaching your children.
2. Build a closer relationship with them.
3. Help them enjoy the learning process.
4. Teach them the joy of the game.
5. Teach them something about the golf swing.
6. Make sure your kids have learned etiquette and the rules.

Teaching should be fun for you. Meeting both sets of priorities should make the process very worthwhile for you and your children.

The best way to teach golf is for the kids to see what you want done and to feel it. Point out only one element at a time, however. Do not fall into the trap of listing every error you see after each swing, or identifying a new error each time. Even with the best teaching technique, overload is a constant threat.

Keep in mind that learning plateaus are common. Regression also occurs. If your children aren't progressing, it's probably a normal part of learning and not something to force or worry about. Make sure you provide positive motivation when the intrinsic reward of learning is not enough. Have them try to hit slices or top the ball, just for fun. Sometimes things won't go well. Provide encouragement when it's needed and the wisdom to stop when it's time.

Perhaps the best way to introduce children to golf is as caddies. Combine a good payday with an occasional swing here and there and you might just turn the mind away from video games for a little while. Being a caddie can be a glimpse into the adult world, a special occasion, a time with Mom or Dad, and, later, fond memories. Bernard Darwin tells the story of one of the most famous of all caddies, 10-year-old Eddie Lowery, who carried for Francis Ouimet in the 1913 U.S. Open:

> He had considerable difficulty in keeping his employer's bag of clubs from trailing on the ground. Mr. Ouimet for the most part held him by the arm and helped him to edge his small way through the crowd. When it came to the last hole, where there is a steep rise before the green, the poor little imp stuck altogether, and had to be almost carried over the crest. He was a most heroic child, and as cool as his master, bearing all the excitement at any rate with outward calm. He had carried for Mr. Ouimet all through the tournament, and when it came to the final fight, someone tried, I believe, by an offer of some dollars to be allowed to take his place; but he stuck firmly to his post and was not seduced. When all was over a band of admirers made up a purse for him, and he went home laden with more dollars than he had ever before possessed.

Can you imagine a kid more proud? And without taking a swing at the ball. This is part of golf, too.

Guiding Principles

Kids are different from adults. Be aware that the brain does not fully develop until the midteens, that emotions are fragile, and that what kids think is funny can be totally obnoxious to you.

The game is supposed to be fun. We forget this in the agonies of our own play, but then, we're used to disappointment. Kids will know in a second when the fun has stopped.

Learning golf should be fun. Although school has drilled out much of the enjoyment of learning, we can return some of it if we approach the task correctly.

Meet children's needs first. Their needs come first and golf's future next; your desires come in dead last. If you don't agree, don't teach.

Children want to learn. The world is full of mystery to them. They are driven to explore, to test, to wonder. Feed them cheerfully.

Children want to please the teacher, sometimes to a fault. Be aware of their dependence, cherish it, and make sure both of you enjoy your time together.

Your job is to find out what your children enjoy and build on that. Know the golf swing well enough that you can recognize it when parts show up and build on them. Let your enjoyment of the game rub off on your kids by enjoying learning together. And last, be a fountain of information turned on or off at will by your children.

Equipment

A beginner requires only one or two clubs to learn the game, but often wants a set anyway. A 3-wood, a 9- and 4-iron (or similar clubs), and a putter make up a good starting set. A glove isn't necessary but a lot of kids have to have them, especially if Michael Jordan or Tiger wears one.

A cut-down set of adult clubs isn't a good idea unless it's the only alternative for a child who really wants to play. They are impossible for some children; they require too much body effort to swing and are both too heavy and too long. The problem is that cutting down adult clubs creates very stiff shafts, making the ball that much harder to hit. This quickly leads to bad swing mechanics and habits. It's also tiring and frustrating. Children require and will enjoy shafts that enable them to hit the ball in the air. Especially for kids under 5 feet, a child's or a soft-flex shaft is best.

Often an overlooked factor in adult clubs, lie angle is especially important for the junior golfer. It is standardized by the manufacturer but can be adjusted to be more upright or flat. Smaller golfers and children often will benefit from a flatter lie angle. As you know, the ball will fly straighter toward the target if the lie angle is correct.

Most children have small and relatively weak hands. Enjoyment and the swing can be improved with smaller-diameter grips. It will be easier for the child to hold the club and release through the ball with a correctly sized grip.

Because of length and loft angles, many beginners can get more distance from a 3-wood than a driver. Doing so makes the game more fun. Make sure your kids have the clubs best suited to their size, strength, and ability.

The more technical issues—shaft flex point, swing weight, forged versus cast clubs, muscle-back versus perimeter-weighted—can wait until kids have an established handicap and an opinion.

Learning the Rules

Games are fun and rewarding only if you follow the rules. Beginning golfers should play to rules, but a different set than experienced players follow. Start your children with rules to fit their ability and maturity, then move toward playing to the official ones at a fairly brisk pace.

One issue is the less-than-accurate counting of strokes. Often children "forget" strokes because it's humiliating to count so many. Religiously counting whiffs and penalty strokes to tally an accurate and honest score is usually punitive and certainly counterproductive. Early on, an accurate counting of good shots—or not counting at all—is more rewarding and encouraging. (Tiger Woods started out with personal "pars" on holes—much higher than normal par). It's a wise teacher who can find something to praise on every hole.

Once children have some competence in hitting the ball, strict adherence to the rules does instill the character for which golf is so famous. As kids become ready, these should be the standard:

- Play golf in a fair and equitable manner. Children see instant replays on television all the time that show an athlete getting away with something. They must learn that golf is different. If you accidentally break a rule and don't call it on yourself, you have cheated and your score is an untruth.
- Every swing at the ball counts. Even adults have trouble with this. Once you know that kids have the ability to hit the ball well, counting everything builds character.

- Avoid gimmies. Nothing is as satisfying as making a putt you think you should make but are afraid you'll miss. Nothing is more dangerous than pretending something is true when it isn't. "I could have made it if I tried" is the summit of a slippery slope.
- Avoid winter rules. Like gimmies, some players have extended winter rules to encompass all but the hottest two weeks of summer. Playing the ball as it lies is in the Scottish tradition and is another way to cope with the inherent unfairness of golf.

Again, strict following of the rules should come only after a degree of competence is achieved. Golf is a pleasurable game—an outing of friends or family. It's fun and rewarding when the rules guide play, but not when they're applied like punches to the nose.

Eight Teaching Points

1. Enjoy the process of teaching your children. If you're not enjoying the process, you can sure bet the kids aren't. If you don't enjoy it, and they don't enjoy it, what's the point?
2. Emphasize balance. Younger ones shouldn't fall away from the ball as they swing. For older kids, balance is one of the keys to a good swing. The head should settle over a flat front foot at the end of the swing.
3. Watch the club hit the ball. No one can see it hit, but this concept keeps the swing centered, smooth, and well balanced.
4. Swing hard. Nicklaus and a lot of others feel that swinging hard is easiest to learn when young. Accuracy can come later.
5. The right hand turns over the left at impact. The full swing doesn't exist without it.
6. Start the downswing smoothly. A generation of golfers was ruined by watching Arnold Palmer lash at the ball. It isn't necessary to strain and puff to hit the ball hard.
7. Stay behind the ball. The more the center of the body moves forward, the more the power of the two levers is lost.
8. Enjoy playing the game with your children. Learn as you teach, and use this time together to get to know one another better—just as you do with your friends.

Perhaps the most revealing reminder of how difficult it is to teach golf well comes from the wife of one of our best teachers. Harvey Penick was excited about his presentation at a PGA convention. "Of all the great teachers, they have chosen me to make this talk," he said, as excited as a kid awaiting a birthday party. "How many great teachers do you suppose will be there?"

His wife gives us all reason to pause and to reflect on how important and how special teaching is. She replied, "I don't know how many great teachers will be there, Harvey, but it's probably one less than you think."

8

THE 19th HOLE

Elitism

Golf is being reduced to the lowest common denominator. Too many people find it too hard to learn and demand easier courses and a more enjoyable pastime. Yes, all of us should have the chance to play, but no one should expect the game to change to meet his particular desires or needs.

Golf values should not be diluted simply because more and more people don't know them. Standards and expectations are higher in golf than in other sports and many other pastimes. Retaining these higher standards is important. Golfers who reach and maintain them are both better golfers and better people than those who don't. We should figure out how everyone can learn, accept, and meet the standards that make golf and many golfers elite in the best sense of the word.

There is nothing wrong with having more players. Progress is a must. In fact, courses should be designed with accessibility for all players in mind, able bodied and not. The Fore All! group in Maryland is doing a great job of providing a course that will be playable by those otherwise unable to participate. The course will be wheelchair accessible, with audible signals for the visually impaired. Numbers and ability aren't what's threatening golf these days.

The real threat, which we must recognize and rally against, is that the essence of the game—pitting your ability and desire against nature and your own frailties—will be lost to a new generation that measures things by how quickly they can be done, how much fun they are, and how little effort they demand. The gift golf gives us is a glimpse of the individual overcoming uncompromising reality: personal, natural, immediate, and not always fair.

Part of golf's decline may be due to the professional game. A hundred years ago professional players were considered second-class citizens, denied entrance to clubs even though they were invited for tournaments. Gentlemen contestants dined under chandeliers in the dining room while professional competitors made do with sitting on the back steps scruffing through handouts wrapped in newspaper. The professionals were a rough, tough gang of sharpshooters, willing to play anywhere, anytime. Today, the pendulum has swung back and conked us on the head.

Televised golfers define what is right and good: Contemplate the shot for a minute or two, go through a belabored preshot routine, stand forever over the ball, look at putts from every angle, and get lined up by the caddie. "Lift clean and place" rules are in effect with every heavy dew. We must guarantee the playing field is level, they say. Take luck out of it; there is too much at stake. It isn't right to take food out of someone's mouth because there's mud on the ball. That wouldn't be fair.

Big money is another threat. Some have seen it coming and have fought the trend. Hord Hardon, protector of the Masters Golf Tournament, was adamant that his invitational would never fall prey to corporate America and become the Pizza Hut Masters. Most other professional tournaments have succumbed, and those that haven't wish they could.

To run a professional tournament, corporate sponsors must be found to guarantee prize money. Organizers, wanting a return on investment, entice name players to participate, often by arranging highly paid outings (or in some places outright appearance fees). Then, of course, they do whatever it takes to secure TV exposure and advertising time. They want some of the money that's in your pocket. That's okay, though. Advertisements are good. You need a car and insurance, you eat hamburgers, and you're going to buy clubs and balls. No problem here.

Except that to sell you something, like a golf club, it has to be better than what you already have and what other club makers provide. The hype begins. Clubs, balls, players, courses, the game itself—all become commodities. Golf's direction is worrisome when:

- Courses charge and get over $300 for a round of golf.
- Sets of clubs can run $1,000.
- Tee times on the Old Course are sold to "packagers" to be resold at a premium.
- Resorts market signature holes featuring greens accessible only by boat, mounds designed to look like women's breasts, and mandatory forecaddies.
- A sleeve of golf balls cost $15 in the pro shop.
- It's cheaper for a family to fly across the state than to play a round of golf together.
- Golf-ball manufacturers spend millions on development.
- Tickets to golf events come only in four-day packets.
- Ruling bodies are afraid to make rulings.

Current and future players are being disenfranchised. High costs are one way; lower standards are the other.

The Spirit

No matter how much we enjoy golf, the game must grow and develop with the times. There is some question, however, as to what can change and what must remain the same for golf to be golf. We may just ruin the game unless we know what to improve and what to leave alone. What is it about golf that makes it wonderful, and what about it needs our protection? This is what Dexter Westrum says in his book, *Elegy for a Golf Pro:*

> Golf is a game as solitary and indefinite as life. When all is said and done, it isn't the score that really matters, and surely, it does not matter whether you beat anybody, because you don't play people, you play the course; but it does matter whether you came off the course with your integrity and your dignity intact. What is important is whether you have submitted your soul to the game.

The best-known golfer in the world is probably Arnold Palmer.* His rugged good looks, charisma, hard-charging

---

*Tiger Woods may be on track to succeed him. Interestingly, Arnold himself challenged his young usurper eyeball to eyeball to take care of the game. Palmer was the featured speaker discussing the future of golf and Woods was in the audience. Palmer's comments were clearly aimed at the young man with influence—and their eyes met as Palmer left the stage and Woods ascended it. So far, Mr. Woods appears to be growing into the position.

shirt-out-of-the-pants swing, and down-to-earth style have won over golfers and nongolfers for decades. Palmer is the quintessential "give your soul to the game" golfer. Fans are aware of his 60 tour victories, his U.S. and British Open championships, his Masters titles, and even his 1954 amateur victory. But few know of the Arnold Palmer Hospital for Women and Children in Orlando or his chairmanship of the national March of Dimes. Arnold has submitted his soul to the game, and continues giving back more than anyone. He signs autographs long after other stars escape to the parking lot. Palmer also understands golf. He knows the game can give and take like a heavyweight boxer. His army has witnessed putts that banged into the cup for miracle comebacks and disasters that leapt out of nowhere. If you see Arnie before, during, or after a round of golf, you can feel the spirit of the man and the game. A good description of giving your soul to the game is playing every time as if the King were your partner.

Irish professional Harry Bradshaw isn't as well known. He was raised, like Palmer, with a reverence for golf, especially the demand for honesty and playing the ball as it lies. Bradshaw led after the first round of the 1949 British Open at Royal St. George's, Sandwich, England. On the fifth hole of the second round, his drive found the rough and, unfortunately, came to rest inside a broken beer bottle. He was aware that relief was possible, but not wanting to delay play by sending for an official, he closed his eyes and smashed at the ball and bottle with his wedge. The ball went no more than 30 yards. He finished with a six on the hole and eventually lost the Open in a playoff with Bobby Locke. Later Bradshaw said he had no regrets; he was beaten by a better player.

Then there was Charles Blair Macdonald, the son of a wealthy Chicago businessman who learned the game while a student at the University of St. Andrews. Although he was behind the development of some of the early American golf courses, he may be best remembered for how he created the need for the United States Golf Association. In 1894 the

Newport Golf Club invited America's best players to a national championship. Macdonald was the heavy favorite among the 20 entered. After opening with an 89, he skied to 100 in the second round of the 36-hole tournament and lost by a stroke. Macdonald complained that important tournaments should be decided in match play, rather than medal. In response the St. Andrews Club in New York organized a match-play tournament a month later. Macdonald was again the favorite of the 28 players in the draw. He lost the finals in a playoff to Laurence Stoddard, then went on to complain that he had been ill and that this wasn't really a national championship anyway. That winter the Amateur Golf Association was born, later to become the USGA. To his credit, Macdonald won the first official national amateur tournament the next year.

The essential difference between Macdonald and Bradshaw is that one was interested in personal glory, the other in doing right by golf.

Perhaps the purest example of the spirit of golf occurred in the 1996 U.S. Amateur final. Fresh-faced Steve Scott was hanging on against the Tiger Woods juggernaut. With 33 holes gone and only 3 to go, Scott was two up. All he needed was to win one or tie two of the remaining holes. On the 34th green Scott's ball was away. Woods marked his ball, then moved his marker out of Scott's line. After putting, Scott watched Woods replace his ball and reminded his opponent to return his mark to its original position, possibly saving Woods a penalty and the loss of the match and the championship. It was a small thing, and a grand gesture. Nineteen-year-old Scott, in the finals of his second amateur, giving his all against the best there was, automatically did the right thing. Scott was battling his heart out, it was the biggest moment of his life, yet the spirit of golf took precedence. This is what must be preserved. No game is like it, and we need to keep it.

The love of golf distinguishes its players from all other sports enthusiasts. But there's much more. There must be an obligation to the integrity of the game, and a sense of giving yourself over to its rules, joys, and torments. Without these things a scratch golfer is only a good golfer, nothing else. There is a code to be followed.

A Canadian tour pro played a casual round at Torrey Pines in San Diego a few years ago. While walking to the green he noticed a candy wrapper tumbling along the ground. Wordlessly he bent over, picked it up, and put it in his pocket. After putting out, he tossed the wrapper into the trash barrel on the next tee. All golfers own the course they are playing, he said. That kind of attitude has many dividends. For one, it helped him play his best. He belonged out there. No one was going to take his place. He had the right to do whatever it took to play well. It also meant that it was his responsibility to make sure the course was the best it could be, for him, his fellow competitors, and the game itself. That included keeping it neat. This professional player also fixed as many ball marks as he could while waiting his turn to putt. He followed the old-fashioned gentleman golfer's code.

Another example is when club professionals visit a course and well-polished courtesies are exchanged. The host accepts the PGA of America membership card as payment in full. The visitor insists on taking and paying for a cart. The host gives the key but often refuses the cash, even though for many club pros cart fees are critical sources of income. Most important is for the visitor to stop in after the round to again thank the host professional for an enjoyable day. Just as when you spend time in someone's home, it's the little things that get noticed and make all the difference.

Young sensation Sergio Garcia did everything right at the second annual Georgia Cup pitting the U.S. Amateur champion against the British Amateur winner. In addition to trouncing the U.S. champion, Hank Kuehne, he further distinguished himself by giving Hank a token gift, a book about his Mediterranean home, and followed that with another presentation to the host club of a porcelain horse from his hometown. Golf is our home and it's a gracious gesture to offer a token of gratitude after spending time in another's house. Garcia did it perfectly.

Invest an afternoon at a golf course observing average players. Take note of the ones who exhibit the spirit I'm talking about. A golf journalist once watched golfers tee off on the first hole of a busy municipal course. The hole was a straightforward par-5, reachable in two by long hitters. There was a bunker and trees on the right, out about 240 yards, and a few trees along the left. Deep rough and a severe drop were just off the tee to the right. Thirty groups went through while he observed.

Quite a few drove into all the trouble short right. Many had bad swings: no wrist cock, no shoulder turn, no follow-through. Some were discourteous, littering, yelling, banging a club on the hole sign; one person drove a cart onto the tee.

Two of the players were notable, however—one a woman, the other a senior man. The woman studied the shot while her companions played, was ready when it was her turn, took a nice swing and hit her 150-yard drive away from trouble, and said a simple "thank you" when praised for her shot. The senior man did pretty much the same, with the added gesture of waving back to the starter as his group turned to walk down the fairway.

That same day the reporter also observed the golfers on the practice green. One man spent 10 minutes adjusting his elementary-age son's hands on the grip and showing him how to accelerate the club through the ball. Finally allowed to putt on his own, the boy's first ball bounded across, then off, the green, followed by the father's yells. The second ball was barely tapped. This pattern repeated itself until the father gave up in disgust to go putt by himself. Meanwhile a teenager dressed in cutoff jeans, a T-shirt, and basketball shoes was earnestly practicing 4-footers. He hit three balls, collected them, and returned to the same spot, over and over. It appeared he was challenging himself to hit so many in a row into the hole. After quite some time he sank 12 in a row, smiled, picked up the balls, and headed to the driving range. A third man was dressed in a white shirt and tie. He putted balls from all over the green in no discernible pattern. His smile was constant, as if putting was the most wonderful thing he could be doing just then.

But the right spirit is much more than just a positive attitude, a simple love of the game, or courtesy. Golf requires dedication, a stick-to-it-until-you-get-it philosophy. Remember how tough it was at first? For most of us, being allowed to accompany Mom or Dad was how the game first revealed its magic. Later, though, there was the struggle to hit the ball well, and a lot of time spent at the driving range and putting green. Not that practice was purgatory, but we dedicated considerable time and effort to learning how to play. Many times there was the declaration that five in a row must be made before the putting green could be left in the growing darkness—or perhaps it was Palmer against Nicklaus.

Golfers find the spirit in the effort to overcome weaknesses and obstacles. The same place Ben Hogan found his genius. Trying, failing, and trying again is the formula for success. Add the joy of sinking a long putt or finally learning how to hit a flop shot, throw in the beauty of the course and a bit of weather, and include the walk to your ball with your best friend and your soul is captured by the game.

Unique Majesty

C an you identify what it is that attracts you so strongly to the game?

Social scientist Brian Stoddart of the University of New England (Australia) suggests investigating the sociological aspects of golf to understand why it arouses such passion, which will then lead to wiser development. He feels that the most significant problems facing the game are not technical but social. Perhaps by understanding the addiction to golf, he says, we may be able to find golfing excellence in all areas.

Collison and Hoskin of the University of Warwick did just that in a paper titled "Discipline and Flourish: Golf as a Civilising Process?" In discussing how man's inherently violent tendencies have evolved in sport, they make an interesting observation: "Following the playing of the first Open in 1860, within fifty years golf had been transformed into an incipient global obsession, and perhaps the exemplary non-violent sport."

They go on to add a concise description of the game that is at risk:

> [Golf] is characterized worldwide by an amateur and "gentlemanly" ethic of self-disciplined behaviour, enshrined in the code of manners known as etiquette and in the extensive and meticulous regulatory framework of rules. It is played in the relaxed pastoral setting of the countryside; players play their own ball and mark each other's scorecards

without direct recourse to an umpire or referee
(even, most of the time, in the professional game
too). There are precise notions of in-group civilised
solidarity in the game's rituals and ceremonies. . . .
Thus one finds, at the heart of contemporary golf,
apparently timeless civilised and civilising traditions, embodied in formal and informal rules and
practices.

Collison and Hoskin add, however, that there are warning
signs that the game is losing this unique majesty. As examples they cite the impact of business in the form of appearance money, the diminishing sense of honor shown by
crowd behavior at recent Ryder Cup competitions, and, on
the amateur level, the ubiquitous sandbagger, improving
lies, and the inability to add up scores higher than seven.
Golf is losing its image and its identity as an honorable
game.

With behavioral science documenting the social benefits for children of such small events as having a meal
with adults, think of the effect a round of golf could have.
The concepts are so powerful: individual responsibility,
no excuses, fixing divots and raking the bunkers, keeping
up the pace of play, warning others of errant shots, calling penalties on yourself, protecting the field, and playing
it as it lies. It is a perspective that builds gentlemen and
gentlewomen, strong of character and strong of will. A
golfer learns that things are sometimes not fair, that some
things are not possible, that anything can happen, and
how to accept, endure, and overcome these realities of
golf and of life.

New standards are always replacing the old. For example, instead of the old way of a golf course being whatever
the land would allow, we have defined a new standard: 18
holes for a full course, commonly with a par of 72, with
clearly defined fairways carpeted with rich green grass, riding carts (preferably the quiet electric ones), and little
chance of lost balls. Over time, what was once simple and

natural—however many holes fit the available land—has become standardized, homogenized, and sanitized. The old standards have become old-fashioned.

Thus the new crossroads become obvious: Just what should our long-term standards be? Should a course have well-defined routes to the green? Should there be equal access to golf for all? Should courses be eco-friendly? Should golf mandate a code of deportment? Should some of the massive money generated by the sport be put to different use, such as development of caddie programs or player education? Should walking be allowed all the time, everywhere? Should there be time limits like in basketball? Should players be licensed to determine access to courses?

Golfers must be wise but at the same time perhaps quixotic, taking on a billion-dollar industry and the momentum of an avalanche of ignorance and greed. Ten golfers will have little effect; nor will a few hundred. But if thousands understand the essence of the game and accept no less, then perhaps, in the immortal words of Arlo Guthrie, "we may have a movement."

A Bygone Era?

G olf isn't doing well at holding our attention compared to other diversions. It's slow, especially next to computer games or punching the TV remote. Even in Scotland, where the game is usually match play, a round takes three hours. In the States, where we must hit our own ball until it finds the hole, quick rounds are those under four and a half hours. The learning curve is both steep and long. Many who could eventually love the game will quit and go off to work on the car or dig weeds in the garden.

From a more global perspective, perhaps society can no longer afford to reserve 100 acres for use by only a few, especially when the chemicals needed to keep it green flow downstream, turning human skin yellow and fish belly-up. Given modern-day demands and expectations, maybe the trend should be to build more pitch-and-putt courses. Most shots are from 60 yards or less anyway, and half the strokes are putts. Artificial greens at a dozen courses already provide a perfectly smooth surface and putt at any chosen speed without all the hassles of mowing, weeding, and pest control. Michael Thomas of *Golf Digest* says that we may be headed toward Japanese-style mass-market golf: the multilevel driving range. Perhaps American know-how could invent new games to make driving ranges fun and make the old-fashioned golf course, and the old-fashioned game, obsolete.

Many changes can be anticipated as golf enters its sixth century. Land for courses is becoming scarce. Developers must search forests, wetlands, and farms for likely sites. Pesticides and fertilizers seep into the water table and drift into schoolyards. Finding a good and affordable place to play will become more difficult.

A serious issue is whether golf is worth all the land it takes to play. The Global Network for Anti-Golf Course Action (GAG'M) is not a spouse's reaction to the Global Golf Nut Network but a serious movement that questions this use of land—especially in Japan, where a full 10 percent of arable land is used for golf. Most people do not play golf and couldn't care less if golfers and golf courses disappeared.

Time is becoming scarce, too. Many people don't play more because of time pressure, such as increasing demands from work and family. Overcrowded courses frequented by untutored golfers take upward of five hours to play. Golf marketers will have to create a quick, simple, and fun entrance to the game. An entry that may not lead to "real golf."

What isn't becoming scarce is information. The USGA's Frank Thomas, who told us that golf is changing, also claims that science can only help. For centuries, he says, golf development has occurred via trial and error. But even with the modern scientific approach, clubs will not be designed that hit the ball 300 yards and always down the middle. Improvement has not been that significant so far, he reports, and this will not change. The benefit of science will instead be that "the consumer is better informed . . . and the rules makers will gain comfort from knowing that they have left no stone unturned to understand and protect the game."

Technology is not the major threat to the game. We are. In the 1990s, according to the National Golf Foundation, a new golf course had to be opened every day to keep up with demand. That's 200 more people materializing out of nowhere every morning ready to play. In 1998, 26 million Americans played 528.5 million rounds of golf. What's needed, most say, is education. If they're not taught otherwise, most of these golfers will play a game that only looks like golf. Teaching the new and disinterested about the joys of golf will retain these new customers so the game will continue to grow. Who can do this? Or, more important, who can do this well enough to pass on the essence of the game to the new generation?

Most sports today do not emphasize the honesty so basic to golf. A 1999 *Seattle Times* article featured cheating as one of the time-honored traditions of baseball, "America's Pastime." At least twice in that year's World Series playoffs a player made an error, miscalled by an umpire, that may have affected the outcome of the game. Neither of the players, at the highest and most visible level of the game, admitted his mistake. Baseball rules don't require that players 'fess up. All the more reason that golf's core values of honesty, honor, and self-reliance must be retained in a sports and cultural environment that focuses almost solely on the value of winning.

One hurdle for golf's core values is that they are no longer rewarding. In the old days these values were the societal norm; following them meant inclusion. Not abiding gentlemanly behavior led to being ridiculed or ostracized. Not so today. An honest person today is a freak or a Boy Scout in knee socks. Find a sack of money in the street? Take it home— it's probably drug money anyway. Many athletes would be hard pressed to choose honesty over being a winner.

Ways to motivate and reward the effort to retain golf's values must be found. We must want or need to do the right thing rather than treating the values as artificial elements of a bygone era.

Keepers of the Game

It is the relationship a player has with golf that creates something more than just a game and someone who plays it. A few enlightened golfers can protect the game, teach others the subtleties and graces of golf, and make sure the changes that come are the best ones. The development of golf will depend on people with vision and influence: those who are Keepers of the Game.

A Keeper of the Game is someone who contributes to golf. Not necessarily on a grand scale either. Keeping the game special can be done in small ways. During your school years, for example, you probably enjoyed a few memorable teachers. These teachers were not educators of international and historic reputation, like a Socrates or a Voltaire. They were just regular people doing the best they could. But they had impact: They added something special to your experience. That's part of what Keepers of the Game are—teachers of sorts, examples, people who add something for other players.

Keepers of the Game embrace golf's core values, including courtesy, respect, discipline, and honor. They improve the game. This could be through something as small as habitually picking up a bit of trash on the course, making the effort to collect old clubs from the garage and giving them to a Junior Golf program, or becoming a member of the USGA. Or it may be on a higher level, like donating to scholarship programs or volunteering time to be on committees.

Keepers certainly do not detract from the game. You won't see them hack a divot and walk off without replacing it, throw a club, or bellow at a 100 decibels if a birdie putt drops. Not that they can't be serious, or even intense—passion is part of the game they love.

The traits of those who will nurture our game include quiet dignity, knowledge, and enthusiasm. Keepers of the Game will be as exceptional as the best courses in the world: strong, natural, beautiful, challenging, and a heck of a lot of fun. The message will be clear yet subtle. Leading by example is the best way.

Noticing the lie of the green while you are pulling your cart to the back of it, for instance, is easily done. Playing companions who must constantly return to the front to collect their clubs will soon catch on. Less subtle but more educational would be giving the flagstick to your fellow player with the comment, "You were first in." Companions will begin to ask questions without even being aware of doing so. You will notice them picking up stray paper in the fairway and digging into their bags for a rulebook, following your silent example.

Even while subtle, you will be clear. What is against the rules, what is not within the bounds of etiquette, what is not within the spirit of the game will not be accepted. It is like protecting the field in a tournament, but in this case, it is protecting the game itself. This can sometimes make a situation difficult. As Patrick Campbell, a British amateur, writer, and baron, noted 50 years ago, "A precise knowledge of the rules [of golf] can earn one a reputation for bad sportsmanship." It's a chance we must take. Part of our task is learning how to educate without becoming disagreeable.

Love of the game does not mean shoving it down other people's throats. We would like willing converts to our movement, not ones shanghaied or browbeaten into submission. A forum for learning is what we are after, an exchange of ideas. After all, golf, once well presented, can stand on its own. Keepers of the Game know that golf is much more than hitting a ball into a hole, and that the essence of the game must not be lost in a world where change outpaces perspective.

You can learn more of this effort by contacting Keepers of the Game. See Resources on page 209.

The Vision

One of the realizations that leads to maturity is understanding that every act has consequences. This is immediately obvious in games, and is one of the reasons we play them. Golf, of course, is one of the most telling. A resting golf ball is safe, a moving one filled with peril, and we made it so. Our definition of the problem and skill in solving it are seen by everyone present in the flight of the ball or its roll along the green. The same is true of golf itself. What we do and don't do has consequences for the game. Our interest is in the character of the golfer and the core values of golf: preserving them, enhancing them, and expanding them beyond the boundaries of the course.

As golf progresses, there will be errors, some serious, others simply fads of little importance. Colored balls are an example of the latter; modern trends in course design may be an example of the former. There are many issues. Is golf etiquette dying? Are there too many high-end courses and too few good low-cost ones? Is the Augusta look taking over? Is there enough encouragement for minorities to play? Are power carts good for the game? Do too few play by the rules?

Get involved. Protect the game. All of your wisdom, knowledge, perspective, desire, and good intentions are meaningless unless you use them to guide golf's development. Unless you actually do something to benefit the game, the game you love may disappear.

Pick a problem and work to fix it.

You may remember that in the semi-olden days, 40 or 50 years ago, tournaments could be viewed from the fairway. There were no ropes strung along cart paths or the rough. Spectators could creep as close to the players as they dared, edging to the fairway, next to bunkers, even along the green. This still occurs at smaller venues, but if you want to see a tour hero up close, your chances are just about gone. The development of stadium courses has carried good intentions to an unfortunate end. Allowing more people to see the game is wonderful—until they have to use binoculars to see the action from the upper deck and a radio to hear it. Golf fans are becoming like spectators of other sports: critical, loud, highly partisan, rooting against good shots. Do you think this trend is going in the wrong direction? Should the golf fan exhibit higher standards than other sports fans?

Junior Golf is great for kids who like to compete but—like Little League baseball—it's too often tarnished by parents and big-time competition. Is there a need for something in addition to the competitive tour for juniors? Perhaps an old-style caddie program to help kids grow into the game? Or maybe courses can take 15 percent off your green fee if you bring a kid to caddie, or to play.

Would you like to see more match play?
Is a 36-hole final day a better test of golf?
Do enough players know the rules? Play by the rules?
Is there trash on your course? Is it noisy?
Are there too many carts? Cart paths in the way?
Should carts be allowed in any tournament?
   Who should be eligible to use them?
Should walking be allowed everywhere?
Does the club pro enhance your game? Does your
   course even have a fully trained professional?
   Do pros make a difference in how the game is
   going to grow? Is it positive? Can they do more?
Does golf really help build character? How do we
   preserve that?

Should the touring player be held more accountable for golf's image?

Does golf need an overall distance standard for all equipment?

Should the big-league professionals play with different equipment?

Who should teach golf?

Should golf be inherently unfair?

Should bunkers be raked?

What is the proper role of ruling bodies, who should be on them, and how much power should they have?

How should golf be modernized?

Scott Stossel in his article "The Golfing of America" (*The New Republic*, 3 August 1998) asks two important questions:

> Will golf, with its rules and codes, its honor system, and its arch regulations of proper behavior, have a civilizing effect on our increasingly crude and unruly culture? Or will the depredations of modern culture drag golf down, infusing it with the boorishness and chaos of modern life?

This volume has addressed these questions. Golf can be a wonderful vehicle to retain and enrich human values through sport. The more people are attracted to the game, the better chance there is to expand golf's values to the larger community. A child who grows up as an honest golfer is also likely to be a good citizen.

Ultimately, there are only three important questions:

1. What do you value in golf?
2. Where do you want the game to go?
3. What are you going to do about it?

If golf is the grand game we think it is, then we need to keep what is important. There is no better game to enhance a friendship or the bonds within a family. Bernard Darwin sums things up well: "It is this constant and undying hope for improvement that makes golf so exquisitely worth the playing." Keepers of the Game are those who will make sure it's done right.

The next 500 years are in your hands.

Open the door to that place where Bob Jones leaps out of a chair to greet you with a strong handshake. Play Cypress Point with Alister MacKenzie. Find a quiet corner and share a whiskey and story with Herbert Wind. Make golf the grand experience it can be. Pursue the knowledge, discover the personal characteristics, and develop the perspective to become a Keeper of the Game. The place is warm and comfortable; there is a roaring fire in the hearth, friendship all around, and a heritage waiting for your name to be engraved.

Resources

BOOKS

Boomer, Percy. *On Learning Golf.* New York: Alfred A. Knopf, 1946.

Brown, Robert. *The Golfing Mind.* New York: Lyons and Burford, 1994.

Cochran, Alastair, and John Stobbs. *The Search for the Perfect Swing.* Grass Valley, Calif.: the booklegger, 1986.

Cochran, Alastair, ed. *Science and Golf.* London: E. & F. N. Spon, 1990.

Cochran, Alastair, and Martin Farrally, eds. *Science and Golf II.* London: E. & F. N. Spon, 1994.

Cochran, Alastair, ed. *Golf the Scientific Way.* Hemel Hempstead, U.K.: Aston Publishing Group, 1995.

Cornish, Geoffrey S., and Ronald E. Whitten. *The Golf Course.* New York: The Rutledge Press, 1987.

Cranford, Peter, G. *The Winning Touch in Golf.* Englewood Cliffs, N.J.: Prentice-Hall, 1961.

Darwin, Bernard. *Mostly Golf.* Edited by Peter Ryde. London: Adam and Black, 1986.

Doak, Tom. *The Anatomy of a Golf Course.* New York: Lyons and Burford, 1992.

Dobereiner, Peter. *The Book of Golf Disasters.* New York: Harper & Row, 1983.

Enhager, Kjell. *Quantum Golf.* New York: Warner Books, 1991.

Farrally, M. R., and A. J. Cochran, eds. *Science and Golf III.* Human Kinetics, 1999.

Hogan, Ben. *Five Lessons: The Modern Fundamentals of Golf.* New York: Simon and Schuster, 1957.

Jones, Robert Tyre. *Bobby Jones on Golf.* New York: Golf Digest Classics, 1966.

Longhurst, Henry. *The Best of Henry Longhurst.* Edited by Mark Wilson. New York: Golf Digest, 1978.

MacKenzie, Alister. *The Spirit of St. Andrews.* Chelsea, Mich.: Sleeping Bear Press, 1995.

McMillan, Robin. *The Golfer's Home Companion.* New York: Simon and Schuster, 1993.

Morrison, Alec, ed. *The Impossible Art of Golf.* New York: Oxford University Press, 1994.

Olman, Morton W., and John M. Olman. *St. Andrews and Golf.* Cincinnati: Market Street Press, 1995.

Penick, Harvey. *Harvey Penick's Little Red Book.* New York: Simon and Schuster, 1992.

Price, Robert. *Scotland's Golf Courses.* Edinburgh: The Mercat Press, 1992.

Rubenstein, Lorne. *Links.* Rocklin, Calif.: Prima Publishing, 1991.

Salmond, J. B. *The Story of the R&A.* London: Macmillan, 1956.

Strawn, John. *Driving the Green.* New York: Harper Perennial, 1992.

Updike, John. *Golf Dreams.* New York: Fawcett Columbine, 1996.

Westrum, Dexter. *Elegy for a Golf Pro.* New York: Lyons and Burford, 1994.

Wind, Herbert Warren. *Following Through.* New York: Ticknor & Fields, 1985.

Wind, Herbert Warren, ed. *The Complete Golfer.* New York: Simon and Schuster, 1954.

Wiren, Gary. *The PGA Manual of Golf.* New York: Macmillan Publishing Company, 1991.

Wodehouse, Pelham Grenville. *The Golf Omnibus.* New York: Bonanza Books, 1991.

PERIODICALS

Golf, New York.

Golf Digest, New York Times Magazine Group, New York.

Golf Journal, United States Golf Association, Far Hills, New Jersey.

GOLFWEEK, Orlando, Florida.

Golf World, New York Times Magazine Group, New York.

Rules of Golf, United States Golf Association, Far Hills, New Jersey.

The New Republic, 3 August 1998, Scott Stossel, "The Golfing of America."

New York Times, 21 February 1999, Lewis J. Horne, "Social Significance of Golf's Evolution."

WEB SITES

www.keepersofthegame.org
www.mrgolf.com
www.popeofslope.com
www.usga.org
www.randa.org

ORGANIZATIONS

USGA, Golf House, Far Hills, NJ 07931, 1-800-336-4446
www.usga.org

National Golf Foundation, 1150 South U.S. Highway 1,
Jupiter, FL 33477, 1-800-733-6006

Keepers of the Game, 3583 Overlook Drive, Langley, WA 98260
keepers@whidbey.com, www.keepersofthegame.org

Royal and Ancient Golf Club of St. Andrews,
St. Andrews, Fife KY16 9JD, United Kingdom